RAISING CAPITAL: THE GRANT THORNTON LLP GUIDE FOR ENTREPRENEURS

RAISING CAPITAL: THE GRANT THORNTON LLP GUIDE FOR ENTREPRENEURS

Michael C. Bernstein

Lester Wolosoff

IRWIN
Professional Publishing®
Chicago • London • Singapore

This publication is designed to provide accurate and
authoritative information in regard to the subject matter
covered. It is sold with the understanding that neither the
author or the publisher is engaged in rendering legal, accounting,
or other professional service. If legal advice or other expert
assistance is required, the services of a competent professional
person should be sought.

*From a Declaration of Principles jointly adopted by a Committee
of the American Bar Association and a Committee of Publishers.*

Senior sponsoring editor: Amy Hollands Gaber
Marketing manager: Tiffany Dykes
Project editor: Denise Santor-Mitzit
Production supervisor: Dina L. Genovese
Assistant manager, desktop services: Jon Christopher
Designer: Heidi J. Baughman
Compositor: Wm. C. Brown Publishers
Typeface: 11/13 Palatino
Printer: Quebecor/Book Press

Library of Congress Cataloging-in-Publication Data

Bernstein, Michael C.
    Raising capital : the grant Thornton guide for entrepreneurs /
Michael C. Bernstein, Lester Wolosoff.
        p.   cm.
    Includes index.
    ISBN 0-7863-0150-3   ISBN 0-7863-1195-9 (paperback edition)
    1. Corporations—United States—Finance. 2. Going public
(Securities)—United States. 3. Corporation reports. 4. Pro forma
statements (Accounting) I. Wolosoff, Lester, II. Title.
HG4061.B47 1996
658. 15—dc20   95–2845

Printed in the United States of America
1 2 3 4 5 6 7 8 9 0 QBP 2 1 0 9 8 7 6

Preface

As a leading international accounting and management consulting firm that specializes in serving growing companies, we often see that entrepreneurs and chief financial officers of these companies need guidance on the capital markets process, particularly on initial public offerings.

Entrepreneurs and business owners need to understand all the capital markets alternatives they have available for meeting their goals. Further, they need to understand what implications, if any, these alternatives could have on their personal estates and corporate assets.

Chief financial officers also often need guidance on developing a business plan as well as an understanding of the accounting and financial reporting implications of the capital markets alternatives.

THE GRANT THORNTON LLP GUIDE

Without a comprehensive guide on raising capital, entrepreneurs often depend on their advisers and friends to evaluate capital markets options. This evaluation process can consume significant time and financial resources. In some cases, costly mistakes have been made because the advice was wrong, misinterpreted, or incomplete.

In addition, growing companies, many of which are privately held, are disadvantaged because information for evaluating capital markets alternatives is not readily available. In particular, accounting and financial reporting implications are often not disseminated for public review.

Raising Capital: The Grant Thornton LLP Guide for Entrepreneurs was developed to satisfy the needs of both entrepreneurs and chief financial officers. Written by partners in the largest accounting firm dedicated to serving midsized and emerging companies, the perspective of the guide's authors is unique.

Grant Thornton LLP's partners understand the challenges entrepreneurs and chief financial officers face in the capital markets process. Further, they are familiar with the full range of financing alternatives available to growing companies.

HOW THE GUIDE IS STRUCTURED

For a company to decide to go public or choose another means of financing, a comprehensive understanding of the going-public process, as well as the available alternatives, is necessary. Our guide was developed to help business owners and managers make informed decisions. It is designed to be a practical how-to book and reference tool. Each chapter begins with an entrepreneur's overview. Illustrative material appears at the end of the chapter.

The guide begins with a look at the capital markets cycle in the early stages (Chapter One). It includes guidance in determining how much money is initially needed, the sources of financing in the early stages, and how to best limit personal liability to the owners and achieve the best tax results.

Chapter Two details how to put a business plan together. Whether a company is going public or using an alternative means of financing, a business plan is necessary. It provides the basis for the company, as well as for underwriters or financiers, to evaluate the company's financial needs and the feasibility of achieving its goals.

Chapters Three and Four walk the reader through the various capital markets alternatives. Among others, private placements, exempt offerings under federal securities regulations, and lending by commercial banks, finance companies, and insurance companies are covered.

Eventually, the decision makers at a growing company will have to decide whether or not to go public. Accordingly, Chapters Five and Six are dedicated to exploring the public securities markets option. These chapters cover issues in preparing to go public, the going-public process, and the postoffering arena.

Chapter Five, on preparing for a public offering, discusses, among other matters, the criteria for selecting an underwriter, attorneys, and auditors; the terms of the letter of intent with an underwriter; the requirements for audited financial statements; and the costs of going public. Chapter Five also outlines the going-public process in detail. The registration process and the typical selling effort are described. The small business integrated registration and reporting system is reviewed and compared to the traditional registration statement on form S-1.

Chapter Six relates the consequences of being public. Requirements for periodic reporting, insider trading restrictions, and proxy rules are discussed.

Chapter Seven describes various other financing sources, such as ESOPs, equity swaps, and franchising. Chapter Eight examines various accounting issues surrounding the going-public process.

At the conclusion of the guide, a glossary of terms is included for quick reference.

ACKNOWLEDGMENT BY THE AUTHORS

Representatives of Rosenman & Colin, one of the most prominent law firms in New York, wrote Chapter Four, *Securities Offerings Exempt from SEC Registration,* and Chapter Six, *After You're Public.*

Representatives of Bear, Stearns & Co. Inc., a leading securities brokerage and investment banking firm, wrote Chapter Five, *Going Public.*

We appreciate the help and insightful views provided by Rosenman & Colin and Bear Stearns & Co. Inc.

We also thank and acknowledge the many partners, managers, and staff members who reviewed and commented on the manuscripts. Finally, we acknowledge and particularly thank our partner, Domenick J. Esposito, who conceptualized this guide and encouraged us to write it.

MORE HELP AVAILABLE

Raising Capital: The Grant Thornton LLP Guide for Entrepreneurs is an important part of the continuing series that Grant Thornton

LLP offers to entrepreneurs and chief financial officers of growing companies. The series also includes:

- Annual supplements for technical and regulatory updates.
- Surveys addressing recent experiences of companies that have raised private and public capital.
- Seminars addressing issues and opportunities with regard to raising capital.

Further information about Grant Thornton LLP's capital markets series can be obtained by writing to:

Mr. Michael C. Bernstein
Partner and Director of Accounting and Auditing
Grant Thornton LLP
605 Third Avenue
New York, NY 10158

Contents

Chapter One

Overview of the Capital Markets Cycle in the Early Stages

ENTREPRENEUR'S OVERVIEW

When an entrepreneur embarks on a new business venture, one of the major concerns is where to obtain the necessary financing. Before beginning the search, he or she must estimate how much money is initially needed.

Other questions to be resolved concern the structure of the new company. Should it operate as a corporation, partnership, limited partnership, or limited liability company? How can the goals of limiting personal liability to the owners and getting the best tax results be achieved? What portion of the investment in the new enterprise should be debt and what portion should be equity?

DETERMINING HOW MUCH MONEY IS INITIALLY NEEDED

An estimate of the money needed during the early stages of a business is necessary because:

- If too little is initially invested, the risk of a halt to operations during the early stages is increased.
- If too much financing is initially obtained, the interest costs and/or the portion of the enterprise exchanged for an equity share will be unnecessarily high.

- The entrepreneur's request for financing will be rejected if he or she doesn't know how much is needed nor has a basis to support the amount needed.

To estimate how much is needed, a cash budget on a month-by-month basis for the start-up period and the first year of operations should be prepared. Typical cash outlays will include legal and organization costs, rent, furniture, fixtures, salaries, payroll taxes, telephone, electricity, insurance, supplies, security deposits, accounting fees, and inventory. Cash receipts from sales or services should also be estimated. Allow for delayed collection of credit sales and for delayed payments to suppliers who grant credit. Include 25 percent of estimated expenditures as an allowance for contingencies such as unforeseen delays in getting started, higher costs than anticipated, overlooked expenses, and optimism in estimating revenues. Revise and update the cash budget at the end of each month.

Estimating revenues, especially for new products, new service concepts, or new markets may be difficult without the aid of an outside market research study. As a business grows and the financing sources become more sophisticated, a business plan will invariably be required. Underlying support for the business plan, including the basis of estimated revenues, becomes more complex. Business plans are described in Chapter Two.

SOURCES OF MONEY FOR A START-UP ENTERPRISE

Founders

Personal assets of the founders are usually the initial source of financing. Savings accounts, loans or mortgages collateralized by equity in the family home and auto, marketable security investments, and loans on cash surrender values of insurance policies are among the available personal resources. Stamps, coins, antiques, paintings, jewelry, baseball cards, and other collectibles are additional resources. Many new businesses start in the home or the garage to save on rent. In a pinch, personal credit cards are used to pay bills for the business. But, if the balances due on the credit cards are not paid timely, the high interest rate can be deadly. Depending on the terms of the plan and subject to certain restrictions, participants may be able to borrow against vested or contributed balances in retirement plans. In addition, a source of reserve funds must be available for personal expenses and emergencies.

Banks

Banks do not like to lend to start-up businesses. A new business has no history of profits and often has no or poor collateral, an inexperienced management, and an inadequate investment by the owners. The bank's risk of not collecting the loan is high. Only a small percentage of start-ups get bank financing.

Leasing

Leasing fixed assets instead of buying reduces initial cash needs. Leased assets require minimal or no up-front cash outlay. The assets that can be leased by a new business are those that are not highly specialized and can be used by others in case of default or at the expiration of the lease. Assets such as autos, trucks, office furniture, and data processing and copying equipment are the types of assets that can be leased by a new business. Although the initial cash outlay is less, the ultimate cost of leasing is usually higher than the cost of borrowing with the asset pledged as collateral.

Finding an Angel or Other Early-Stage Venture Capital

Individuals with money to invest, referred to as angels or business angels, are sources of equity capital in the start-up or early-growth stage. An angel's investment may range from $10,000 to several hundred thousand dollars. However, larger amounts up to and in excess of $1 million have been invested by one or more angels. Lawyers, accountants, other entrepreneurs, and bankers are potential referral sources to angels.

There are computerized services and venture capital clubs that match start-up businesses with angels. Lists of each of these matching sources are published in *Money Sources for Small Businesses* by William Alarid (Puma Publishing Co., 1670 Coral Drive, Santa Maria, CA 93454). The same publication lists venture capital firms that are interested in investing in start-ups.

The *Corporate Finance Sourcebook*, published annually by National Register Publishing Company, 3004 Glenview Road, Wilmette, Illinois 60091, catalogs sources of capital funding, including venture capital funds, private lenders, banks and commercial financing, and factoring firms. The catalogs include industry and geographic preferences; whether investments are preferred for seed capital, start-ups, or companies in a more mature stage; minimum and preferred sizes of investment; and other lending criteria. (Seed capital is intended for companies that have an idea but that have not started a business; start-ups are nearly ready to begin operations or are in an early stage of operations.)

Classified ads in *The Wall Street Journal* (Thursdays), *The New York Times* (Sundays), or other local papers placed by businesses seeking investors and by persons or organizations looking for investment opportunities can also create leads to financing.

The minimum that venture capital firms invest is usually significantly higher than the minimum that an individual angel invests. Venture capital firms require a more formal business plan or proposal.

Other Sources

Relatives and friends are sometimes willing to invest or lend, although it may ultimately result in a strained relationship. Suppliers will, at times, provide short-term financing and/or give extended credit terms to a new customer. On occasion, a customer of the new venture, seeking a new source of supply, will provide financing.

Government Sources

A vast number of federal, state, and local programs provide advisory and financial assistance to qualified businesses. The Small

Business Administration (SBA) is a principal source of federal assistance.

A substantial majority of SBA loans are made under its guaranteed loan program. The business submits a loan application to a lender (mainly a bank). If the lender approves, it submits the application to the SBA. If the SBA approves, the private lender makes the loan, which the SBA guarantees. The SBA can guarantee up to a maximum of $750,000.

Under an SBA direct loan program, the maximum available is $150,000, and it is usually available for special classifications such as businesses owned by low-income or handicapped persons.

The objective of these programs is to help businesses that can't get a loan elsewhere. An applicant can be declared ineligible if money is available on reasonable terms from sources other than the SBA. (Other sources include proceeds from the sale of assets not necessary for its business or growth.) The direct loan program requires, depending on capitalization size or the area, one or two rejections by banks as a prerequisite.

Businesses can be a good size and still be considered eligible for SBA-supported loans. For example, as a rule, the number of employees at a manufacturer cannot exceed 500, but some manufacturers can have as many as 1,500 employees and still be eligible. Maximum revenues can range as high as $22 million for certain wholesalers. Size limitations are determined by industry classifications.

Other conditions include the following:

- Sufficient collateral is required. Personal assets of the principals will be used if assets of the business are not sufficient.
- Personal guarantees of principal owners and the chief executive officer are required.
- Nonprofit organizations (with exceptions for such nonprofits as cooperatives or sheltered workshops employing the handicapped) are ineligible.
- Funds cannot be used for certain activities, including publishing, relocation costs, gambling, or lending as a primary business.

Small Business Investment Companies (SBICs) are privately owned businesses licensed by the SBA to provide equity and long-term debt to businesses below stipulated sizes. By pledging to finance small businesses, SBICs become eligible to get long-term loans from the SBA.

SBICs vary with regard to whether they prefer to make loans or equity investments, the industries they prefer to finance, and their minimum and maximum investments.

Minority Enterprise Small Business Investment Companies (MESBICs) are similar to SBICs but can only fund minority-owned businesses.

Other federal programs are administered by various agencies. They include a Small Business Innovation Research Program, various programs providing financing to companies in certain specific industries, and programs such as disaster relief. There are myriad state programs that offer a wide variety of assistance to businesses.

Brief descriptions of federal and state programs and the names and addresses of the pertinent agencies administering the programs are included in *Money Sources for Small Businesses* by William Alarid. The same book also includes lists of the names and addresses of SBICs and MESBICs.

Government-Sponsored Advisory Services

Regional Small Business Development Centers (SBDCs) provide information for new business owners. Volunteers of the Service Corp. of Retired Executives (SCORE) offer counseling assistance and low-fee workshops for small-business owners. Call (202) 205-6766 for the name of the nearest SBDC and (202) 205-6762 for the nearest SCORE chapter.

DETERMINING THE LEGAL FORM

A business can be operated as a sole proprietorship, a general partnership, a limited partnership, a corporation, or a limited liability company. A newer concept enacted in a handful of states is the Registered Limited Liability Partnership. For tax purposes, a corporation, if eligible, may elect to be treated as an "S corporation." The two key considerations in making a choice of legal form are concerns for potential liability of the owners for unpaid business debts and the tax consequences of the different choices.

Personal Liability Consequences

In a general partnership, two or more people operate a business in an unincorporated form. The partners are personally liable for the full amount of partnership liabilities.

In a sole proprietorship, the sole owner, operating in an unincorporated form, is personally liable for all business debts.

In a limited partnership, certain designated partners, referred to as limited partners, may limit personal liability up to the amount of their investment in the partnership. A limited partnership consists of one or more general partners and one or more limited partners. Limited partners cannot be active in the management of the business.

Corporate stockholders are not normally liable for corporate debts unless they assume specific responsibility, for example, through personal guarantees. The corporate stockholders can therefore also limit liability up to the amount of their investment. Personal liability from certain activities, such as the practice of medicine, law, accounting, and architecture, cannot be avoided by the use of the corporate form. The limited liability partnership alleviates, to a degree, liability resulting from these activities.

The use of a corporation, instead of an individual, as a general partner in a limited partnership can, in many cases, shield the individual(s) who own stock in the corporation from personal liability. Personal liability to the general partners can also be shielded by agreement with the creditors. An example is the case of a nonrecourse mortgage, in which the lender agrees to look only to the property pledged as collateral for recovery and not to any other assets.

Almost all states have authorized a new form of entity, the limited liability company (LLC). The limited liability company limits the liability of a member to the member's investment. It may, depending on whether it has fewer corporate characteristics than noncorporate characteristics, as defined in the tax code, qualify for tax treatment as a partnership.

Tax Consequences

For tax purposes, there may be a choice to elect S corporation status for a corporation. Among the criteria for the election of S corporation status are the following:

- There can be no more than 35 shareholders.
- No shareholder may be another corporation, a partnership, or a nonresident alien.
- Only certain types of trusts may be shareholders.
- The S corporation may not be a member of an affiliated group, as defined.
- The S corporation may only have one class of stock (under certain circumstances, debt could be considered another class of stock).

If the S corporation status is broken or revoked, it cannot be reinstated until five years after termination.

The general partnership, the limited partnership, and the S corporation pass profits through to their partners or shareholders. Losses also pass through to the owners, who, subject to limitations, including the passive activity loss and the at-risk provisions, may net off such losses against income from other sources.

Stockholders of S corporations cannot deduct losses in excess of their investment and loans to the S corporation nor provide for non–pro rata allocations of profits and losses. General partners have an advantage over S corporation shareholders because the limitation on their deduction for losses includes their share of the partnership's liabilities to nonowners, as well as the partner's investment and partner loans to the partnership. In addition, profits and losses can be allocated, if the partnership agreement so provides, in proportions other than in accordance with the partners' interests in the partnership, provided the allocations have "substantial economic effect." The criteria for substantial economic effect include requirements that when a partner's interest is liquidated, liquidating distributions must be made according to the partner's positive capital account balances and that a partner with a deficit balance in his or her account after liquidation is obligated to restore the amount of the deficit in the partnership. In effect, the partner who pays for the losses can deduct them, even if the losses are not in proportion to the ownership interests. The initial year(s) of operations usually anticipates losses. Therefore, investors providing the cash for their interest may, subject to the passive activity loss limitations, prefer a limited partnership as a means of sheltering income from other sources.

The C corporation (any corporation that is not an S corporation) is subject to a separate tax on its earnings. The stockholders are also taxed when the earnings are distributed. Losses of the C corporation are not available to be offset against the stockholders' income from other sources. Losses can generally be offset against corporate taxable income in profitable years (carried back three years or forward 15 years).

As for the limited liability company (LLC) whose members are not personally liable for the company's debts, the Internal Revenue Service may classify as a partnership those LLCs that have a majority of corporate characteristics. As a result, the limited liability company may combine the benefits of a pass-through entity with limited liability. A ruling as to the company's tax classification would be advisable. The partnership classification of an LLC would mean that the members are subject to the at-risk and passive loss rules. Limited liability companies, as contrasted to S corporations, are not restricted to 35 shareholders, can have more than one class of stock, are not limited as to type of shareholder, and are eligible to file consolidated returns if they own more than 80 percent of another corporation or are more than 80 percent owned by another corporation. LLCs are also able to make special allocations of profits and losses similar to partnerships, provided the allocations have substantial economic effect. As indicated before, almost all states have limited liability company laws. There is some uncertainty about qualifying a limited liability company for partnership status. Further, liquidating an existing corporation to convert it to an LLC will result in taxes to the corporation and its stockholders on any excess of the fair market value of the corporation's assets over the basis of its stock.

If organized as a corporation that meets the requirements as a "small business corporation" under IRS Code, Section 1244, at the time the stock is issued, loss on the sale, exchange, or worthlessness of the stock is deductible, within limits, as an ordinary loss by individuals (or a partnership) who were the original purchasers. The aggregate ordinary loss is limited to $50,000 on separate individual returns and $100,000 on joint returns. Losses exceeding the limitations are treated as capital losses. In order to qualify under Section 1244, the corporation must not have received in excess of $1 million for capital before the shares are issued. Section 1244 stock must be issued for money or property other than stock, securities, or services. Since an S corporation will have previously passed through its losses, the advantages of Section 1244 stock to the shareholders of an S corporation are usually less important.

Summary

In the desire to avoid the specter of personal liability for the owners, there is a tendency for start-up businesses to select the corporate form of operating the business. If eligible, the election as an S corporation can combine the limited liability with a pass-through of early-year losses to the owners (subject to the passive activity and at-risk rules). However, as a pass-through entity, the limited partnership has additional latitude to allocate losses on a non–pro rata basis, the advantage of limited liability of the limited partners, and the ability to shield liability of the general partners by the use of a corporate general partner if the corporate general partner has substantial net worth.

The LLC may become the vehicle of choice since it can combine the more attractive features of pass-through entities and limited liability protection without such S corporation limitations as who can be shareholders or the number of shareholders.

During profitable years, the avoidance of the double tax, initially at the corporate level and then at the individual level when earnings are distributed by the corporation, is another advantage of a pass-through entity. This advantage still exists in most cases despite the increase in individual income tax rates by the 1993 Revenue Reconciliation Act.

Because of the complexity of the rules and the diverse circumstances that may exist, it is important to discuss the issues with your tax adviser.

DEBT VERSUS EQUITY

In federal tax law there are advantages in the treatment of debt where the corporate format is used.

- Interest on debt is deductible, whereas dividends on equity are not deductible.
- The repayment of debt principal is treated as a return of investment, whereas payments on stock redemptions will first be treated as dividends to the extent of existing earnings and profits.
- A loss to the investor on worthless debt may be treated as a bad debt, creating an ordinary deduction rather than a capital loss.

The standards for determining whether debt owed to owners will be considered equity for tax purposes are not clearly defined but include factors such as:

- Whether the debt is an unconditional promise to pay a fixed sum at a fixed interest rate on a fixed maturity date.
- Whether the debt-to-equity ratio is too high. Generally a three-to-one or four-to-one ratio is acceptable.
- Whether the debt and equity holdings are proportionate.

From a financing point of view:

- More debt results in a worse debt-to-equity ratio, which makes it more difficult to obtain additional debt financing.
- Interest expense reduces net earnings (or increases losses), which is detrimental to getting financing.
- Interest payments deplete cash needed for growth.

In the early stages, when losses are anticipated, interest deductions on loans from the investors are wasted by the C corporation, while resulting in taxable income to the investor. For financial statement purposes, the interest expense increases financial statement losses, and the debt has an adverse effect on the debt-to-equity ratio. In a pass-through entity, the interest reduces earnings on the financial statements and has an adverse effect on the debt-to-equity ratio; but, for tax purposes, the increased loss resulting from the interest deduction will offset the interest income to the partners. There appears to be no advantage to creating debt through the founder(s) investment in the early stages; however, some investors, such as friends and relatives, may want the priority of a debt investment plus the interest income.

Consultation with your financial and tax advisers is recommended.

Appendix
ILLUSTRATION OF TAX CONSEQUENCES—PASS THROUGH ENTITY VERSUS C CORPORATION

	C Corporation	S Corporation	Partnership
Income	$500,000	$500,000	$500,000
Stockholders' salary	(250,000)	(250,000)	—
Distributions	—	—	250,000
Taxable income to business entity	$250,000	Not relevant (a)	Not relevant (a)
Tax to business entity	$80,750(b)	$ —	$ —
Taxable to stockholder or partner			
Salary	$250,000	$250,000	$500,000
Passed through	N/A	250,000	$500,000
	$250,000	$500,000	
Tax to individual	75,529(b)	174,304(b)	174,304(b)
Total initial tax	156,279	174,304	174,304
Tax to individual assuming distribution of retained earnings as dividend	46,234(c)	—	—
Total ultimate tax	$202,513	$174,304	$174,304

Appendix *(continued)*

Notes:

(a) A pass-through entity does not pay federal income taxes on its income. The partners are taxed on the partnership's income, and the income of an S corporation is taxed directly to its shareholders. Undistributed income increases the basis of the investment to the partners or shareholders of the S corporation.

(b) Based on rates enacted under the 1993 Revenue Reconciliation Act. The 1994 rates for married filing joint returns were used for the stockholder or partner individual returns calculations. The individual's calculation assumes no other income nor any credits or deductions.

(c) Distribution of retained earnings by a C corporation to the shareholder and tax to the shareholder in a subsequent year.

Earnings before income taxes	$250,000
Corporate income taxes	80,750
Available for distribution	$169,250
Tax to individual shareholder	$ 46,234

The tax at 1994 rates for married filing joint return assumes no other income to shareholder nor any credits on deductions. If the shareholder's income in the year the distribution is received is greater than $250,000, the tax on the $169,250 distribution would be $67,023.

If the shareholder sells his or her stock at a gain equal to the undistributed earnings, a capital gains tax at 28 percent will be paid if the stock has been held for more than one year. The capital gains tax (in this illustration, $47,390) could therefore be less than if earnings are distributed as dividends when the individual reaches higher tax brackets.

The highest taxes ultimately result when the C corporation is used. It would take about 10 years with a net return of 10 percent on the initially lower tax under the C corporation to equalize the ultimate lower tax under the pass-through entities.

The estate of a C corporation shareholder who holds the stock until death, without a dividend distribution, could get the stock at the date of death value, thereby avoiding the income tax on dividend distributions. This assumes that the accumulated earnings tax (which is not imposed on pass-through entities) does not become a problem to the C corporation during the shareholder's lifetime.

Chapter Two

Business Plans

ENTREPRENEUR'S OVERVIEW

Purposes of the Business Plan

The emphasis of this guide is the procurement of outside financing. Lenders or investors require a business plan in most situations before considering whether to lend or invest.

There are, however, other important management reasons for preparing a business plan over and above obtaining financing. During the course of preparing the plan, management will find potential problems. Corrective measures can be taken in advance and the problems avoided. A plan also communicates to all management levels the goals expected to be met. The plan can be further used as a comparison to the actual results. Differences between the plan and the actual performance can highlight areas where changes are required to improve operations or to modify the plan itself if original goals were unobtainable.

Variances, especially unfavorable ones, between the plan and actual operations will draw questions from lenders and investors. Unexplained variances from industry norms for projected gross profit margins, growth patterns, and other relationships will also strain lender and investor belief. Therefore, the plan's projections and goals should be realistic in order to maintain credibility.

Format and Contents

Contents and emphasis of the business plan will vary depending on factors such as the industry; whether the plan is for a manufacturer, a service company, or a retailer; and whether the enterprise is in the development stage, is an established business, or is seeking to make an acquisition. There are no "boiler plate" plans. Even companies in the same industry and at the same stage of development have different strengths, risks, and needs. Each business plan should be custom-made.

The sections included in the business plan typically fit within the following captions:

    I. Executive Summary
   II. Description of Company, Products, Technology, and Industry
  III. Production Process
  IV. Marketing
   V. Management Team
  VI. Risk Factors
 VII. Financial Data
VIII. Potential Acquisitions
     Appendices:
      1. Organization Chart
      2. Management Résumés
      3. Market Survey
      4. Price Lists
      5. Photo(s) of Product(s)
      6. Fixed Asset Acquisition Schedule
      7. Historical Financial Statements
      8. Projected Financial Statements

The cover to a business plan should include the name of the company, its logo (if any), the address, the phone number, and the name and title of the person to be contacted. The name of the lender or investor and the date of submission should also appear on the cover page. A statement at the bottom of the cover page should state that the information appearing in the business plan is confidential and should not be copied, distributed, or disclosed without the consent of the company. A table of contents and a list of attachments or appendices should follow the cover page.

Don't flood the market with unsolicited copies. Contact should be made with the potential financing source before submitting the plan. If possible, submit the plan to three or four potential sources at a time, to avoid delays if turned down one at a time and to get a basis for comparison of available terms. Inquire as to special information requirements of each source.

The lender or investors will probably obtain credit reports on the company, its officers, and directors. Before submitting the plan, the company should obtain these credit reports and have inaccurate information corrected.

EXECUTIVE SUMMARY

Investors and lenders receive and read many business plans. They screen applications to weed out unlikely financings. A concise, informative executive summary, as the first section of the plan, is important. It may be the deciding factor as to whether the investor or lender gives further consideration or rejects the financing without reading the rest of the plan. Some investors will request to see a proposal before getting the whole plan. A well-prepared executive summary can serve as the nucleus of a proposal.

The summary, normally one to three pages in length, should have enough detail to permit a lender or investor to make a preliminary evaluation. It is usually written after the main sections of the plan are completed. Brief discussions of topics such as the following are typical:

- The company's industry and whether it is in the start-up, development, or established-business stage.
- Company products or services and advantages of the products or services.
- Market potential.
- Background and role of the management and other key executives.
- The amount and proposed uses of the financing.
- The length of time that such financing is expected to satisfy the company's requirements.
- The source and estimated time of payback.
- Collateral available.
- The estimated rate of return to an investor (if equity financing).

- Equity and debt invested by existing shareholders.
- Condensed three-to-five-year historical financial highlights:

     Working capital.

     Property, plant, and equipment.

     Other assets.

     Long-term debt.

     Equity.

     Net revenues or sales.

     Net earnings or loss.

- Cash generated from (used in):

     Operations

     Investing

     Financing

- Disclosure of unusual or nonrecurring items.
- Condensed three-to-five-year projected financial highlights (prepared with the assumption that financing is obtained and the funds are expended as planned).

     Working capital.

     Property, plant, and equipment.

     Other assets.

     Long-term debt.

     Equity.

     Net revenues or sales.

     Net earnings or loss.

- Cash generated or used from:

     Operations

     Investing

     Financing

- Disclosure of key assumptions or factors underlying the projections, particularly in changes from the historical financial results.

DESCRIPTION OF COMPANY, PRODUCTS, TECHNOLOGY, AND INDUSTRY

Size and Ownership

Indicate the size of the company in terms of its revenue and number of employees. Describe who owns and controls the company and for how long they have controlled the company.

Operating History and Industry Background

Describe the company's business or industry. State its rate of growth and reasons for such growth. Briefly describe acquisitions. State the company's fundamental goals and how it expects to achieve them.

Product Function and Technology

Describe the principal products and their uses or technology. Indicate the product life cycle and potential for obsolescence, if that is a factor. Set forth the trademarks, copyrights, and patents held by the company, the extent to which they are key to the business, and their expirations.

Advantages of Products

Set forth the advantages of the company's products or services such as:

Ability to be produced or sold cheaper.

Protection afforded by copyrights or patents.

Features that have unique benefits or appeal to customers.

Research and Development

List planned new products and their uses or technology. Relate anticipated competitive advantages of the new products. Describe the stage of development of the new products. Set forth the estimated time and cost to complete their development. Indicate if prototypes exist.

PRODUCTION PROCESS

The following items, when pertinent, should be included in a narrative of the production process.

- Indicate where the plant(s) is (are) located and state the size in terms of footage.
- Enumerate or describe significant equipment, including age, condition, and technological factors.
- Specify plant and equipment under lease and describe terms of the major leases, such as rent, expiration date, renewal options, and so forth.
- Describe any advantageous features, such as below-market rentals, favorable location in relation to the market, shipping facilities, and labor force.
- Discuss the consequences, if any, of changing technology.
- Discuss the adequacy of existing facilities to meet goals established by the business plan.
- Detail plans for adding to the plant and equipment and estimated costs.
- Describe the manufacturing or service process and the use of contractors, if any.
- Discuss the availability of raw materials and the ability to replace sources of supply if such becomes necessary.
- List key suppliers.
- Discuss the size of labor force, the level of skill required, availability, and labor relations.
- Discuss inventory management and production techniques, such as just-in-time systems and electronic data interchange.
- Discuss quality control and industry standards.

MANAGEMENT TEAM

The plan should discuss the background of the principals, officers, sales manager(s), production manager(s), research people, any other key employees, and directors. The following should specifically be disclosed about each: (1) age, (2) percentage ownership in the business, (3) length of time with the company, (4) duties, (5) prior business experience, (6) compensation, and (7) any employment contracts.

The objective is to demonstrate the experience and capabilities of management and key employees in the major areas, such as marketing, production, research (if pertinent), and finance. If some of the expertise comes from outside consultants, they should be included in describing the management team. Outside consultants include attorneys, accountants, market research firms, production consultants, and so forth. Outside directors are expected to provide oversight, and their backgrounds and outside experience should therefore be included.

An organization chart and management résumés should be among the exhibits included in the appendices.

MARKETING

Current Market

Describe the size of the market and the enterprise's share or rank in the market. Indicate geographic areas where the products are sold.

Describe the characteristics of the company's customers and where they are located. Characteristics would include customers' industry and whether customers are service organizations, manufacturers, or governmental agencies. If sales are to retail consumers, significant characteristics would include items such as age group, sex, income levels, and other demographic data.

List the major customers. Indicate their industry if the product is used in more than one industry. Include the percentage of the company's sales to these customers.

Competition

Describe in general terms who competes with the company. If there are dominant competitors, list them. Compare the advantages and disadvantages of the company in relation to its competitors. Information as to who the competitors are can be obtained from directories such as *The Thomas Register of American Manufacturers,* an annual publication of the Thomas Publishing Company. The *Register* lists manufacturers by product manufactured. The Dun & Bradstreet, Inc., *Million Dollar Directory* lists 50,000 companies that meet certain size criteria and includes a directory of businesses by industry following the standard industrial code (SIC Code) system.

If the competitor is public, Form 10-K (Annual Reports) or registration statements can be obtained from brokers, the Securities and Exchange Commission, stock exchange libraries, directly from the public company, or from enterprises that provide such data for a fee, such as Disclosure, Inc., and SEC on Line. Extensive details about privately held competitors may be harder to get, but a subscriber to the Dun & Bradstreet credit reports can obtain data from a credit report.

Industry data can usually be obtained from trade associations or trade publications.

Potential Market

Size of potential market and projected market share. State the estimated size of the potential market and the company's projected market share.

Determining whether there is a market for a new product or expansion is a difficult task for many individual entrepreneurs and family-run businesses. Market research is usually beyond their expertise. In addition, running the business day to day leaves little time for such research. Many existing businesses get by on little or no market research and obtain financing for new ideas or expansion based on experience, prior success, and quality of collateral. But many companies do not have such experience or collateral. Even companies that get financing without business plans should prepare business plans for the management reasons previously noted. The projected revenue is the starting point from which the projected net earnings and cash flow are calculated. A sound basis for estimating market potential is important. Retaining an outside market research firm or a consultant to determine if there is a demand for the product, especially as it relates to international markets, and to estimate the enterprise's share, could be money well spent.

With the large increase in the availability and sophistication of computer databases, a certain amount of market data can be obtained by outside firms at a relatively low cost.

If a market research firm or consultant is still not affordable, business libraries contain industry directories, publications, and databases as well as U.S. government statistics that should enable an enterprise to establish a basis for estimating the existing and potential market. Trade associations are also a source of market data and growth estimates. The Small Business Administration has available publications and videotapes on how to research demand for a product or service.

Potential Customers

Describe who the potential customers are, their characteristics, and where they are located. For example, the customers might be persons in a particular age group who live in urban areas and have achieved certain educational levels. Indicate the size of the customer base and the rate of growth. State the basis for these statistics, such as a market survey and/or industry publications or directories.

Pricing

Discuss the pricing and its relationship to the customers' decision to buy. Either the customer will pay the price because of the unique qualities of the product or because of the competitive nature of the price. If the prices are projected to be lower than the competition, indicate what the expected reaction of the competition will be and how that may affect your ultimate share of market. Estimate the effect on profitability if less than the targeted share of market is achieved at planned prices. State the sales dollar break-even point (described in a subsequent section of this chapter). If a market research study was performed, describe customer sensitivity to price.

Distribution

Indicate the distribution channels used and whether the company will use salespeople or sales agents who act as representatives for several companies. Describe the qualifications of the sales force. Also describe planned special channels of distribution, such as the use of specialty stores versus general department stores. Relate what customer services are provided to enhance the product's appeal.

Promotion and Advertising

Describe promotion and advertising plans. Indicate the media historically used, to be used, and the budget for each. Describe the media used by the industry and compare the company's plans to industry norms.

FINANCIAL DATA

Historical Financial Statements

Some lenders or investors require historical financial statements for three years. Others require five-year financial statements. The financials are typically included among the exhibits in the appendices. The main section of the plan provides analyses of the financials and might include:

- A discussion of revenue trends with an explanation of the causes of the growth or decline in revenue.
- A comparison of gross margins for the years included, with an explanation of the causes of significant variances from year to year.
- A review of the earnings trend, with an explanation of items causing significant variances from year to year.
- A table setting forth key financial ratios, with an explanation of variances between years.
- A comparison of the company's financial ratios to industry ratios (obtained from sources such as the Robert Morris Associates' *Annual Statement Studies* or Dun and Bradstreet's *Industry Norms and Ratios*).

Financial Ratios

Ratio	*Formula*	*Description*
1. Gross Margin	Gross profit ÷ Net sales	An assessment of management effectiveness in controlling costs and pricing policies.
2. Receivables turnover	Accounts receivable at year-end ÷ (Credit sales ÷ 365)	A measure of the average time in days that receivables are outstanding; can indicate collection problems.
3. Inventory turnover	Cost of sales ÷ Average inventory	Can indicate overstocking or obsolescence.
4. Current ratio or working capital ratio	Current assets ÷ Current liabilities	An indication of a company's ability to meet its immediate obligations.
5. Acid test or quick ratio	(Cash + Marketable securities + Current accounts receivable) ÷ Current liabilities	A more conservative indication of a company's ability to meet its immediate obligations.
6. Debt to equity	Liabilities ÷ Net worth	Measures size of risk assumed by creditors relative to risk assumed by owners.
7. Return on equity	Net earnings ÷ Net worth	A measure of management effectiveness (although a high rate of return could indicate undercapitalized company).
8. Times interest earned	Earnings before interest and taxes ÷ Interest expense	Indicates company's ability to pay interest and borrow further.

Projected Financial Statements

Projections are usually for three years and hardly ever longer than five years. The projected statements should include projected balance sheets at each projected year end, statements of earnings, and statements of cash flows for each projected year. The first and second years should be projected on a quarterly basis. The third (and any subsequent years) should be projected on an annual basis. The projected financial statements are normally included as an exhibit in the appendices. The projections should include disclosure of the key assumptions concerning the bases of the projected sales, the cost of sales, research and development costs, selling expenses, general and administrative expenses, interest (including estimated interest rates on debt financing being sought), amortization of goodwill (if the plan includes proposed acquisitions), depreciation (including capital expenditures planned and described in the discussion of facilities), and income taxes.

Disclosure of assumptions relating to the statement of cash flows should include assumed terms for collection of receivables, terms of payment of payables, cash received from the planned financing, repayment of debt, uses of proceeds from proposed financing, and expected inventory levels.

The projected balance sheet is derived by adjusting the balance sheet at the beginning of the year for the transactions reflected in the projected earnings and cash flow statements. Assumptions for projections should not contradict goals stated in the business plan.

Break-Even Analysis

It is useful to estimate how much in sales are needed before the company would break even after adding a new product or expanding existing product lines. The break-even point is computed by dividing fixed costs by the contribution margin. The contribution margin is calculated by dividing the unit sales price minus the variable cost per unit by the unit sales price.

The calculation requires: (1) separating costs into fixed (those costs that do not vary with sales levels) and variable (those costs that do vary with sales levels), (2) accumulating total additional fixed costs projected for the new product line, (3) setting a sales price per unit, and (4) calculating the variable costs per unit.

To illustrate the calculation, assume that: (1) the projected fixed costs for a new product are $300,000, (2) the estimated unit sales price is $8, and (3) the estimated variable costs per unit is $6. The break-even volume is computed as follows:

Fixed costs $300,000 ÷ Contribution margin of .25
= $1,200,000 Break-even volume

The contribution margin was calculated by subtracting the variable cost per unit, $6, from the unit sales price, $8, and dividing the result, $2, by the unit sales price.

Many costs are partially fixed and partially variable. Further, at different levels of sales volume, costs that were fixed may vary. Despite the limitations resulting from the inexactness in categorizing expenses as fixed or variable, the break-even analysis provides a useful yardstick in evaluating the risk associated with new products.

Sensitivity Analysis

Assumptions whose variance is reasonably possible and would significantly affect the results of the projections are particularly sensitive. Disclosure of the potential effects of the variations or presenting two projections, one at the expected results and the other based, for example, at a lower sales level, may lead to a better understanding of the feasibility of the plan.

Rate of Return to Investors

Investors' expectations of the return on investment depends on the extent of risk as viewed by the investor. The higher the potential risk, the greater the expected return. The following factors affect risk and should be considered so that there is an awareness of what rate of return the investor seeks:

- Established products with an existing market are less risky than new products or ideas for products without an established market.

- Single product companies represent greater risk than multiproduct companies.
- A large investment by existing owners reduces risk to new investors as it indicates the entrepreneur's commitment to the venture.
- A well-rounded management team represents less risk than a single entrepreneur.

Depending on the relative risk, a venture capitalist who makes only an equity investment expects a return of 40 percent per annum and up. Recoupment of the investment is generally expected through public offering or acquisition by another company.

As an example, a venture capitalist who invests $2.5 million would need to sell the investment for approximately $13.5 million at the end of five years to realize a 40 percent return compounded annually. The investee company projects earnings for the fifth year of $2.5 million with a projected earnings multiple of 15. The total market value of the company is projected to be $37.5 million ($2,500,000 multiplied by 15). The venture capitalist would require a 36 percent interest in the company ($13,500,000 divided by $37,500,000) to realize the 40 percent rate of return.

RISK FACTORS

Risks should be disclosed with management's opinion of the outcome and an explanation of the effects. Examples of disclosure risks are:

Negative Cash Flows, Accumulated Deficits, and Working Capital Deficiencies

Reference should be made to the business plan and how the strategy contemplated by it is projected to reverse the negative trend. Indicate the time period projected for the recovery.

Government Regulations

Describe:

- Significant segments of the business that may be subject to renegotiation of profit or termination of contracts or subcontracts at the election of the government.
- The status of compliance with issues raised by federal, state, and local environmental regulations.
- Pending approvals of products or licenses by agencies such as the FDA or the FTC.
- Significant investigations by agencies such as the SEC, FDA, or IRS.

Litigation

Describe pending legal proceedings other than routine litigation incidental to the business.

Products Liability

Describe any unusual situation that may reasonably develop into a significant problem.

ACQUISITIONS

If the financing is needed to make an acquisition, the business plan should include additional information about the proposed acquisition as follows:

- Historical financial statements of the company to be acquired.
- Purpose of the acquisition and how it will improve earnings and/or the cash flow of your enterprise.
- Background of management of the acquired company that will stay on after the merger.
- Pro forma combined historical statements for the last year as if the two companies had been combined. Such pro

formas would give effect to amortization of stepped-up bases of assets, increased interest costs (of debt financing), savings resulting from contemplated retirements, salary reductions, restructuring, and so forth. (Note that for SEC purposes, pro forma adjustments for contemplated savings are permitted only under certain circumstances, but such information may still be appropriate for a business plan.)

- Projected financial statements on a combined basis with key assumption disclosures and key ratios.
- Marketing strategy and marketing techniques of the acquired company and how it will affect (if at all) the acquiring company's marketing.
- Production process of the company to be acquired.
- Risk factors relevant to the acquired company with management's opinion of the outcome and an explanation of the effects.

Appendix
A SAMPLE BUSINESS PLAN

A sample business plan for a company in the development stage that is looking for equity financing follows. Material listed as part of the appendices is not included.

BUSINESS PLAN

METROPOLITAN POLYMER, INC.

932 Flower Hill Road

Hoboken, New Jersey 08830

Address Inquiries and Communications to:

Mr. Ronald Shaus, Treasurer

1

CONTENTS

Executive Summary

The Company
  Background
  Products
  Industry Background

Production Process
  The System
  Sources of Supply
  Properties
  Research and Development

Marketing
  Marketing and Sales
  Competition
  Patents and Trademarks
  Potential Market

Management Team
  Outside Directors

Financial Data
  Historical Data
  Projections
  Key Assumptions

Appendices
  Organization Chart
  Market Survey
  Management Résumés
  Fixed Asset Acquisition Schedule
  Historical Financial Statements
  Projected Financial Statements

Government Environmental Regulations

2

EXECUTIVE SUMMARY

Metropolitan Polymer, Inc. (the "Company"), was organized in 1991 to engage in the plastics recycling business through the manufacture and sale of various products produced from plastic scrap utilizing an extrusion-molding process. The Company has utilized its process to manufacture products from plastic scrap such as fencing, boardwalk planking, industrial pallets, picnic tables, and park benches that are marketed and sold under the trademark "Polyproducts." The Company is in the start-up stage and its revenues to date have been limited.

The Company has also been engaged in upgrading the design and engineering. The completion of the upgrading of the design and engineering, which the Company anticipates will occur in mid-1994, is expected to enable the Company to expand its manufacturing operations and to improve the quality and variety of its products.

Its process, as currently constituted, gives the Company the ability to manufacture its products at lower costs than other companies that recycle plastic waste. Although Polyproducts are more costly than similar products made from wood, metal, or concrete, they are stronger, have a longer life, and are more durable than the products made from traditional materials.

The demand for the Company's products and technology is growing as a result of public concern and government pressure to deal with solid waste disposal problems. Efforts to encourage plastics recycling on the state and local level, such as "bottle bills" and other regulations that require separation of plastics from solid wastes and the collection of plastic waste, have had a significant impact on both the availability of raw materials and the public's sensitivity to products manufactured from recycled waste.

The existing demand for the Company's estimated share of the market is supported by a market research study conducted by New Market Research Corp. (see copy in the appendices).

Mr. Moore, the Company's President, and Mr. Willis, the Vice President of Production, own 60 percent and 30 percent, respectively, of the Company's stock. Both were key to the growth and profitability of National Plastics Furniture, Inc., a publicly held

3

manufacturer of plastic furniture. Mr. Moore was chief operating officer and, before that, marketing director, and Mr. Willis was production manager of National Plastics Furniture. Mr. Shaus, the Company's Vice President of Finance, has extensive experience in planning, budgeting, and finance.

Because of its competitive advantages and the experience of its executives in the plastics field, the Company believes it has an extraordinary opportunity to take advantage of the emerging market.

Based on its detailed financial projections, the Company proposes to sell a 37 percent equity interest for $2,500,000. The funds will be used in order to complete the upgrading of the design and engineering of its manufacturing process and to finance the initial marketing and sales efforts, the development of new products, and to provide sufficient working capital until a positive cash flow is generated.

If the Company receives its anticipated equity financing, it projects a positive cash flow from operations and profitable operations in the third year after the financing. Thereafter, depending on market conditions, the Company plans a public offering of its common stock for the benefit of its shareholders and to provide funds for additional expansion.

Highlights of projected operations for each of the five years ending June 30, 1998, are as follows:

	Year Ending June 30,				
	1994	*1995*	*1996*	*1997*	*1998*
		(In thousands of dollars)			
Sales	$10,000	$15,000	$22,000	$26,000	$33,000
Net earnings or (loss)	(110)	(235)	1,100	1,400	2,500
Cash generated or (used)	1,670	(285)	1,050	1,350	2,450

The above results are based on the assumption that the proposed sale of a 37 percent equity interest is completed during the year ending June 30, 1994. See the section on Financial Data and the projected financial statements appearing among the appendices for other key assumptions and further details.

THE COMPANY

Background

The Company was organized in 1991 to engage in the plastics recycling business through the manufacture and sale of various products produced from plastic scrap, utilizing an extrusion-molding process.

In 1991, the Company acquired substantially all of the component assets comprising its extrusion-molding process, as well as other equipment, located in Hoboken, New Jersey. Since the acquisition, the Company has produced products manufactured from plastic scrap, such as fencing, boardwalk planking, industrial pallets, picnic tables, and park benches that are marketed and sold under the trademark Polyproducts.

The Company has also been engaged in the upgrading of its production facilities. The completion of the upgrading, which the Company anticipates will occur in mid-1994, is expected to enable the Company to expand its manufacturing operations and to improve the quality and variety of its products.

At June 30, 1993, the Company had 16 employees. Three are the executive officers, six are production and engineering personnel, five are sales personnel, and two are administrative.

Products

The Company manufactures various lumber-like products from commingled consumer and industrial scrap. The Company's products, which are sold under the trademark Polyproducts, are designed to resist damage or destruction caused by weather, water, fungus, rot, and insects for applications in areas that are particularly prone to such damage or destruction. Polyproducts can be used in fresh or salt water, and above, below, or on the ground, without having to be painted or treated, and can be recycled. The Company anticipates that products made of Polyproducts will be sold for use in industrial, agricultural, recreational, and marine engineering areas.

The extrusion-molding process enables the Company to cast a variety of shapes, including the curved ends of park benches and picnic tables. The molded parts can be square, round, rectangular, oval, tapered, or irregular to fit many specified applications. Polyproducts can also be fabricated using conventional woodworking and machine-shop tools. Polyproducts are produced in a variety of colors.

Industry Background

During the last decade, the consumption of plastic products in the United States has grown significantly. Industry sources estimate that the plastics industry produces over 50 billion pounds of plastic annually, yielding significant percentages of usable wastes. The growing use of plastic has caused the public and government to become concerned about its disposal. Until recently, used plastic has typically been disposed of by burial in landfills or by incineration. The closing of landfills, public resistance to incineration, and related environmental concerns have created the need to dispose of industrial and consumer scrap and waste plastics through recycling rather than traditional methods. In response to the concerns about disposal of plastic waste, there has been an increase in state and local government regulation and development of incentive programs for solid waste disposal. As a result of such regulation and programs and the concerns surrounding plastic waste disposal, a plastics recycling industry has emerged that is attempting to solve disposal problems and find economic uses for recycled plastic waste.

Recycled plastic is becoming an increasingly important source of material for many commercial uses, and, in certain cases, replaces traditional materials such as wood, concrete, and metal. Moreover, the Company believes that the increasing supply of

6

plastic waste, the variety of products into which it can be formed, and the increased emphasis on government-sponsored recycling programs will create significant opportunities in the plastics recycling industry.

PRODUCTION PROCESS

The System

The extrusion molding process, acquired in mid-1991, consists of: (1) nonproprietary component equipment and machinery used in the plastics process and (2) proprietary know-how, including a method of configuring the nonproprietary equipment, which allows the Company to mix, extrude, and fabricate the plastic waste into usable products.

All plastic waste is reclaimed by separating the waste by type of plastic and granulating such waste into small pellet-sized pieces. The plastic pellets are mixed with other types of plastic and fillers for extrusion. During the extrusion process, the plastic mixture is melted and injected into molds of varying sizes and shapes, depending on the final product. The design of the process permits the utilization of custom-designed molds for products of different shapes and sizes.

The finished products are removed from the molds for cooling and, if required, may be assembled into finished products with ordinary woodworking methods for products such as park benches or picnic tables, or may be shipped directly to customers in unfinished form, such as fence posts, planks, or plastic lumber.

The Company intends to use a portion of the net proceeds from this financing to continue to upgrade the design and engineering of the process, to improve its speed and efficiency, and to purchase new equipment.

The equipment and machinery utilized are commercially available.

The completion of the upgrading of the design and engineering, which the Company anticipates will occur in 1994, is expected to enable the Company to expand its manufacturing operations and to improve the quality and variety of its products.

7

Sources of Supply

The Company uses both consumer and industrial plastic waste in its recycling and reclamation business. The Company's consumer plastic waste comes primarily from municipal recycling centers, and its industrial plastic waste is purchased from a range of industrial manufacturers, plastic processors, and bottling companies. Although the Company is not party to any supply agreement, the Company believes that adequate supplies of plastic waste are available at acceptable prices.

Properties

The Company's executive offices and manufacturing facility are located at 932 Flower Hill Road, Hoboken, New Jersey. The property consists of 22,000 square feet and is leased until May 31, 1998, at an annual rental of $45,000. The Company has the option to purchase this facility at any time during the lease term at a price of $400,000.

Research and Development

During the years ended June 30, 1993, and 1992, the Company expended approximately $200,000 and $150,000, respectively, on research and development efforts in connection with the development of products. Approximately $200,000 of the proposed financing will be used for such purpose.

MARKETING

Marketing and Sales

The Company intends to sell its products directly to certain specialized industry accounts and through manufacturer's representatives throughout the United States. The Company's marketing

8

efforts for its products will be primarily conducted by its President and Marketing Director, Joseph Moore. He will be assisted by the Company's market consulting firm, New Market Research Corp. A copy of the market study is included in the appendix. The Company intends to use a portion of the proceeds of this financing for its marketing and sales efforts, including market research and advertising in trade magazines and other print media.

Sales to Flexiboard, Ltd., and Technique, Inc., during the year ended June 30, 1992, represented approximately 15 percent and 12 percent, respectively, of the Company's revenues. The Company is not, however, dependent on sales to these two or any other single customer.

Competition

In the sale of its products, the Company competes directly with companies that recycle commingled plastic waste. The Company believes that there are no dominant competitors. In the opinion of management, the Company's process gives it technological superiority, resulting in competitive advantages.

Products manufactured by the Company from commingled plastic waste compete with similar products made from traditional materials, such as wood, metal, and concrete. Although the Company's products are more costly than similar products made from traditional materials, the Company believes that it will be able to compete with manufacturers of products made from traditional materials, primarily on the basis of advantages, such as strength, projected longer life, and durability of its products.

Patents and Trademarks

The Company's existing process is comprised of items of equipment that are not proprietary to the Company. However, the Company considers the know-how underlying the process to be proprietary. The Company does not have any patents with respect to its process. The Company relies on unpatented know-how and trade secrets. The Company plans to use a portion of the proceeds from this financing to upgrade the design and engineering of the

9

process, which the Company believes will improve its speed and efficiency.

The Company's products are marketed under the trademark Polyproducts and the Company regards such trademark to be proprietary. The Company has filed an application to register such trademark with the United States Patent and Trademark Office.

MANAGEMENT TEAM

The Company's executive officers are:

Name	Age	Position
Joseph Moore	52	President and Marketing Director
Edward Willis	44	Vice President of Production and Director of Research and Development
Ronald Shaus	40	Treasurer

Joseph Moore, a cofounder of the Company, has been its President, Marketing Director, and a member of the Board of Directors since the inception of the Company. Prior to that, he was President and Chief Operating Officer of National Plastics Furniture, Inc., a public company that manufactures plastic furniture, for 10 years and the National Director of Marketing for six years prior thereto. From 1964 to 1977, he was employed in various capacities, including four years as Northeastern regional sales manager for Bowl-O-Soup Company. Mr. Moore has a B.A. degree from Fordham University.

Edward Willis, a cofounder of the Company, has been its Vice President of Production and Director of Research and Development and a member of the Board of Directors since the inception of the Company. Prior to that, he was employed by National Plastics Furniture, Inc., in various capacities, including that of Production Manager from 1984 to 1991. Mr. Willis has a B.S. degree in Mechanical Engineering from Northeastern University.

Ronald Shaus is a CPA with over 15 years of experience in accounting and finance. He joined the Company in October 1991 and has served as a member of the Board of Directors since that date. From 1988 to 1991, he was Treasurer of Soul Shoe Corp., a public company that manufactures women's shoes. He previously served as Controller for Desktops Inc., which operates retail computer stores. Mr. Shaus began his career with Grant Thornton LLP in 1975. He has a bachelor's degree in Business Administration from C. W. Post University.

Outside Directors

Charles Mayer has been the President of See Thru Toys, Inc., a developer and manufacturer of plastic toys for young children for more than 20 years.

Thomas Maio is a retired CPA and former senior partner in a regional CPA firm. He is a director of several publicly held companies.

In addition, New Market Research Corp., a consulting firm, has performed a market research study for the Company and has been engaged to provide marketing research and consultation on an ongoing basis.

The Company's attorneys are Abel & Corruthers.

The Company's independent public auditor is Grant Thornton LLP.

The compensation of the key executives and ownership of the Company's shares is as follows

Name	Ownership (%)	Compensation
Joseph Moore	60%	$125,000
Edward Willis	30	100,000
Ronald Shaus	2	75,000
Other investors	8	—

Mr. Moore and Mr. Willis each have five-year employment contracts, expiring in 1998, for an annual salary of $125,000 and $100,000, respectively. Under the terms of the contracts, Mr.

11

Moore and Mr. Willis will be entitled to an annual bonus of 3 percent and 2 percent, respectively, of earnings before income taxes in excess of $1,000,000.

FINANCIAL DATA

Historical Data

The Company was formed in May 1991 and is in the development stage. Revenues have been limited to date. During the years ended June 30, 1993, and June 30, 1992, the Company sustained losses of $490,000 and $370,000, respectively. As of June 30, 1993, the Company had a stockholder's equity of $155,000 and working capital of $300,000.

Projections

Highlights of and key assumptions for the projected financial results for each of the five years ending June 30 are as follows:

	Year Ending June 30,				
	1994	1995	1996	1997	1998
	(*In thousands of dollars*)				
Working capital	$ 1,970	$ 1,685	$ 2,735	$ 4,085	$ 6,535
Property, plant, and equipment (net of accumulated depreciation)	1,400	1,200	1,000	800	600
Other assets	175	175	175	175	175
Long-term debt	1,000	750	500	250	—
Equity	2,545	2,310	3,410	4,810	7,310
Sales	10,000	15,000	22,000	26,000	33,000
Net earnings or (loss)	(110)	(235)	1,100	1,400	2,500

12

	Year Ending June 30,				
	1994	*1995*	*1996*	*1997*	*1998*
	(In thousands of dollars)				
Cash generated from or (used in):					
Operations	$ (30)	$ (35)	$ 1,300	$ 1,600	$ 2,700
Investing	(800)				
Finance	2,500	(250)	(250)	(250)	(250)
Total cash generated or (used)	$ 1,670	$ (285)	$ 1,050	$ 1,350	$ 2,450

Key Assumptions

Sales. The market study performed by New Market Research Corp. indicates that the Company's potential share of the existing market is approximately $45,000,000 a year. The sales projection assumes that the upgraded equipment, scheduled to be completed in fiscal 1994, will be able to operate at full capacity for an entire year in fiscal 1995. It reflects estimates of a projected growing market and the Company's projected increased percentage of the market, as described in the complete market study included among the attached appendices.

Cost of Sales. Because of increasing state and local governmental recycling requirements, the supply of available materials is expected to increase with a resulting reduction in unit price. Labor is also expected to be readily available with minimal cost of living increases estimated over the five-year period ending June 30, 1998. The projections include provision for additional plant employees to be added as production increases. Manufacturing overhead includes depreciation of the $800,000 equipment upgrade completed in 1994, which will not result in an increased unit cost because of the expanding volume of sales.

13

Because of the reduced material cost and insignificant labor and overhead cost increases, projections reflect a gross profit of 30 percent throughout the five-year period.

Selling Expenses. The projections reflect promotion and advertising cost increases of $200,000 a year for each of the four years ending June 30, 1998. Expenses that vary, such as selling commissions, are based on sales volume.

Research and Development. The projections anticipate expenditures for research and development of new products as follows:

June 30,	Amount
1994	$100,000
1995	200,000
1996	200,000
1997	100,000
1998	100,000

Officers' Salaries. The salaries of the President and the Vice President are reflected at $225,000 a year, the aggregate amount stated in their employment agreements, plus bonuses of 3% and 2%, respectively, of earnings before taxes in excess of $1,000,000.

Break-Even Point. The Company estimates that operations will break even when sales reach $16,000,000.

GOVERNMENT ENVIRONMENTAL REGULATIONS

The Company's recycling operations are subject to federal, state, and local environmental laws and regulations that impose limitations on the discharge of pollutants into the air and water and establish standards for the treatment, storage, and disposal of wastes.

The Company believes that it is in substantial compliance with the governmental regulations and that environmental compliance for its operations will not entail significant costs.

15

Chapter Three

Debt Financing

ENTREPRENEUR'S OVERVIEW

Debt or Equity

From the enterprise's point of view, equity capital is permanent capital invested by the owners. Debt is viewed as temporary, with a promise to repay specified amounts at future dates. However, many debt instruments have features that give them some of the characteristics of equity, and some equities have debt-like characteristics.

Depending on an investor's or lender's goals, required repayment or redemption provisions; required payments of interest or dividends; covenants that place restrictions on the issuer; preference in liquidation; voting rights; and the right to share in the growth of the company either through conversion rights or warrants to buy common stock are attractive characteristics. The issuer, while considering the objectives of the investor in order to obtain the investment or loan, would like to limit these features.

Preferred stock and common stock are the legal forms of equity capital. Preferreds, more typically than common, have the characteristics of both debt and equity. The debt characteristics can include features such as required redemption, cumulative dividends (not required payments, but payable before common dividends are paid), and liquidation preference over common (but junior to debt). Debt can include such equity features as convertibility to common. Subordinated debt is considered equity by some senior lenders. A debt is subordinated when there is an agreement, in the event of liquidation or bankruptcy, to repay the debt only after obligations to other creditors, usually certain specified creditors, are satisfied.

Some managements borrow the most they possibly can. In profitable years, the high leverage increases the return on investment. However, the decision to issue equity securities is often the solution thrust upon an enterprise because its debt levels are too high and it cannot borrow more. Further, interest rates may be too low and/or fear of inflation may be too high to enable an issuer to complete a debt financing.

Pros and Cons

Advantages of borrowing include:

- Interest payments are deductible for tax purposes; dividends on equity securities are not deductible.
- There is no dilution of the existing common shareholders' interest. However, debt that is convertible into common stock has the potential to dilute the common stockholders' control (common stockholders ordinarily have the right to vote) and share in the company's growth and appreciation.
- Preference over stock in liquidation and the required payments of interest and repayments of principal may be attractive characteristics to certain investors.
- Because of market or other conditions, it may not be feasible to raise equity capital at a time when the company's debt levels are already too high. If some existing debt can be subordinated or if new subordinated debt can be raised, additional conventional debt may become obtainable because, as indicated, subordinated debt is considered equity by some senior debt holders.

The advantages of raising funds through equity issuances are:

- It does not have to be repaid (except when the corporation is obligated to redeem the stock—most frequently redeemable preferred).
- There are no required dividend payments (except that cumulative preferred stocks require that prior unpaid

preferred dividends must be paid before any common stock dividends are paid).

• Failure to pay dividends does not constitute a default. Failure to pay the interest or the principal of the debt as scheduled constitutes a default that can lead to a loan becoming currently due and payable.

• There are no restrictions by way of negative covenants that accompany most long-term loan agreements and many short-term loan agreements. However, equity placed with private investors will usually be accompanied by some restrictions.

• Unless the issuer is required to redeem it, proceeds from the sale of stock is included in the equity section of the balance sheet. (Public companies cannot include redeemable stock in equity unless the redemption is solely at the option of the issuing corporation.) Increasing equity improves financial ratios and makes the incurrence of additional debt easier.

Preferred stock issues can be advantageous insofar as certain features may have appeal to certain investors.

• In liquidation, claims of preferred shareholders rank ahead of common shareholders.

• Holders of convertible preferreds, in exchange for a lower yield, have an opportunity to share in the company's growth and appreciation.

• Dividends have a fixed rate of return; however, there is no requirement to pay dividends, except that unpaid prior-period dividends on cumulative preferred stock have to be paid before any dividends can be paid on common stock.

• A corporation with surplus funds to invest may opt to invest in preferreds that pay dividends rather than bonds because it can reduce taxable income by 70 percent of dividends received from unaffiliated domestic issues. Interest from corporate bonds is generally taxable in full.

DEBT FINANCING

Debt is divided for accounting purposes between short-term debt, payable within one year, and long-term debt, payable after one year. From a financing point of view, debt is generally thought of as short term, due in less than a year; intermediate term, maturing after one year and up to five years; and long term, maturing from 5 to 25 or 30 years. The most commonly used debt-financing instruments, their sources, and terms are described in the following sections.

Lines of Credit

Under a line of credit, a bank agrees to lend up to a specified maximum amount at any one time. The business borrows under the line when necessary and repays it when the money is no longer needed. The purpose of the line is usually to meet seasonal buildups of receivables and inventory, which are pledged as collateral. In addition to interest on the borrowed amount, a commitment or standby fee is often charged on the amount of the line not borrowed. The line of credit is evidenced by notes that are due on demand or that mature in 30 to 90 days. The lines of credit are regularly renewed (rolled over). In many cases, the bank expects the line of credit to be paid up for one or two months each year. Banks will often require that a specific percentage of the line be borrowed and maintained as a compensating balance in a noninterest-bearing account with the bank. The required compensating balance can range up to 10 percent of the amount drawn on a line of credit. The source for repayment of the line of credit is the sale of inventory and collection of receivables that build up during the season.

A business that cannot periodically pay down its line and is constantly rolling it over will obtain a revolving line of credit (revolver) that has a longer-than-one-year maturity. Compensating balances are usually required. Revolvers are often repaid from the proceeds of a term loan or an equity financing.

Asset-Based Lending

Asset-based lending involves debt financing that is collateralized by accounts receivable, inventory, plant and equipment, or real estate. Asset-based lenders are known as commercial finance companies. Commercial finance companies will lend to businesses that cannot obtain adequate financing from banks. However, most banks and some major industrial companies have divisions or affiliates that perform the same functions.

The commercial finance company primarily bases its loan approval on estimates of ability to realize the collateral in the event of a forced liquidation. As a result, assets with no liquidating value, such as prepaid expenses or those that would be difficult to liquidate (i.e., highly specialized equipment) are not considered adequate as collateral for asset-based lenders. Inventory and receivables (as with a regular line of credit) are the most liquid and therefore the most frequent form of collateral for revolving loans. Fixed assets usually serve as the basis for term loans.

Although emphasis is placed on the realization of collateral, projected cash flow from operations is not overlooked in the loan evaluation, as it serves as the first source for repaying the loans.

Commercial finance companies generally do not require compensating balances.

Factoring

Factoring involves the sale of accounts receivable rather than the pledge of receivables as collateral. The factor performs a credit check of the enterprise's customers and approves sales in advance. For efficiency, credit limits for regular customers may be preapproved in advance. The factor does not have recourse to the company for uncollected amounts except for credits arising from defective goods, returns, or disputes. Under a notification agreement, the invoices to the customers contain a notice that the receivable has been sold and that payment should be made directly to the factors. If receivables are sold on a nonnotification basis, payments from customers are usually directed to a bank lockbox under the factor's control. Depending on the arrangements, monies are remitted to the company either when the invoice is due, whether paid or not (maturity factoring), or when the merchandise is shipped (nonmaturity factoring). Under nonmaturity factoring, interest is charged by the factor from the date of the advance to the due date of the invoice.

A fee, the factoring commission, is charged for the assumption of the credit checking, collection functions, and the credit risk. A portion of the monies due will be held back to pay for the factor's commissions and fees and to serve as a reserve for returns, allowances, and discounts.

The sale of receivables usually results in their removal from the balance sheet, and no loan for their financing appears. If pledged as collateral, the receivable remains on the balance sheet, and a loan payable is included as a liability. The sale of receivables therefore results in improved current and debt-to-equity ratios. As a result of the improved ratios, debt financing may become feasible, and negative loan covenant violations may be avoided.

Leasing

The use of property and equipment can be financed through a lease instead of borrowing to buy the asset. In the past, the advantages of leasing included certain tax benefits and, for financial presentation purposes, the ability to avoid recording a liability for the amounts borrowed to finance the purchase. Many of the tax benefits were eliminated by legislation in 1986, and the ability to avoid reflecting a liability for leased assets was restricted by accounting rules published in 1976. However, there may still be benefits to the use of leases as a means of financing the acquisition of property or equipment.

- The down payment in the form of advance rentals required under a lease is usually smaller than the equity investment required when the asset is purchased. This is an important consideration for an enterprise that is short of cash.
- Not all assets under lease have to be capitalized with a corresponding liability recorded. The basic rules require

capitalization by a lessee when it meets any one of the following criteria:

1. The lease transfers ownership of the property to the lessee by the end of the lease term.
2. The lease contains a bargain purchase option.
3. The lease term is equal to 75 percent or more of the estimated economic life of the leased property.
4. The present value of rental and other minimum lease payments equals or exceeds 90 percent of the fair value of the leased property.

Criteria 1 and 2 are not applicable when the beginning of the lease terms falls within the last 25 percent of the total estimated economic life of the leased property.

Leases that do not meet any one of the above criteria are classified as operating leases, and no capitalized asset or liability need be reflected. Lease terms are sometimes structured so that they do not meet the criteria for capitalization, even if it results in an economic disadvantage to the lessor. Avoiding capitalization results in improved financial ratios that can, at times, be the determining factor in not violating a loan covenant or in obtaining additional debt financing.

- Short-term cancelable leases protect the business from the risk of obsolescence, although the rents for such leases will probably be high.
- Special equipment that will be used for a relatively short term are more economical to lease than buy.
- The problem of disposing or selling used equipment is usually avoided.

Costs of leasing versus purchasing should be compared. One method is to compare the present value of the after-tax cash outflows of leasing and buying. Comparisons should also be made between different leasing and buying proposals. The interest rate used in such computations should be the company's borrowing rate. Although the initial cash outlay is usually lower under a lease, the cost of leasing over the term of the lease is usually higher than purchasing.

Banks, independent leasing companies, and finance subsidiaries of equipment manufacturers are the prevalent sources of lease financing.

Commercial Paper

Commercial paper is unsecured short-term notes issued by larger enterprises that usually have excellent credit ratings. Maturities are less than a year, ranging from 30 to 270 days. The issuer ordinarily obtains a line of credit to back up the commercial paper at maturity in case it cannot roll over the commercial paper or meet the obligations when due. Depending on the maturity terms of the underlying line of credit, the commercial paper can be classified as a long-term debt on the balance sheet.

The commercial paper is sold at a discount. The interest rates are normally lower than bank lines of credit rates, and there are no compensating balances. Most paper is rated by Standard & Poor's or Moody's and is sold through commercial paper dealers.

Securitization

Securitization refers to the process of pooling similar receivables to turn them into debt securities. The receivables provide the cash flow necessary to repay the debt that they "back up." Receivables arising from automobile loans, leases, mortgages, and credit card transactions are types of assets that have been used to provide the means of repaying the underlying debt. The process may, in the future, be applied to trade receivables. The borrower can obtain a lower interest rate because the cash flow from the securitized assets usually represents a better risk than the borrower's overall credit rating.

The securitized assets that back the debt have to be identified and segregated on the records of the borrower. Normally, a trust is formed to own the pool of receivables to be securitized. Investment bankers assist in grouping the assets, for example, by maturities to correspond to different needs of investors. In recent years, income-producing real estate properties have also been pooled to back up bond offerings.

Term Loans

Term loans satisfy the intermediate-range financing needs and are often packaged with a revolving line of credit whose purpose is to meet the seasonal needs.

Repayments are customarily required over the term of the loan, with the final payment due three to five years after the original amount is borrowed. Payments, including interest, are mostly quarterly or semiannual. If the scheduled periodic payments are not enough to fully pay the principal over the term of the loan, a balloon payment is due at the maturity date. At maturity, the balloon is usually refinanced.

Mortgages

A mortgage is a long-term note used to finance the acquisition of, and is collateralized by, a specific piece of property. The property can serve as collateral for a first, second, or third mortgage note. A first mortgage is senior to the second, which is senior to the third. When the down payment and the funds available from a first mortgage are not enough to pay for the property, the seller may decide to accept the remaining balance on credit by taking a second mortgage position. A mortgage note given to the seller is referred to as a purchase money mortgage.

A mortgage is either paid off over its life through periodic payments (self-amortizing) or is paid down to a specific amount, leaving a balance (balloon) still due at the maturity date. Although the general credit and cash flows of the borrower are important, appraisals are necessary, as repayment in the event of default is dependent on the property, especially if it is undeveloped. Where the loan is nonrecourse, the lender cannot look to the credit of the borrowing enterprise for recovery in the event of default, but only to the property. Interest rates on nonrecourse financing are usually higher than for recourse financing.

Borrowers will refinance and prepay a long-term loan when interest rates drop. To protect the lender, prepayment is usually not permitted for a specified period after the loan closing, and a penalty for prepayment, when permitted, is charged.

Depending on how specialized the property is, mortgage financing is usually available up to 70 percent of the value of the property and for a term up to 20 or 25 years.

Bonds

Bonds are long-term notes with a maturity of 10 or more years and have the following characteristics:

- Interest is expressed as a percentage of the face amount. Debenture bonds are uncollateralized.
- Coupon or bearer bonds have detachable coupons that are presented at the interest due date for payment. The ownership of coupon or bearer bonds is not registered by the issuer.
- Bonds are sometimes guaranteed by the parent of the issuer or an affiliated company.
- When portions of bonds mature at different dates, they are referred to as serial bonds. Payment is made at face value on a prescheduled basis.
- A bond loan agreement (indenture) may require that annual payments be made into a sinking fund that is used to purchase the bonds.

Private placement of bonds has the following advantages over a public offering:

1. Issuance costs are lower, especially for smaller issues.
2. Registration with the SEC is not necessary.
3. If the corporation is not already public, costs of periodic filings, and so forth, can be avoided.
4. Problems such as difficulty in making payments can be more easily resolved.

On the other hand, the private buyer of the bonds is in a better position to negotiate restrictions on the borrower.

Zero Coupon Bonds

Zero coupon bonds and variations thereof are sold at a very deep discount and pay no interest. The difference between the discount price and the maturity value represents the yield. The borrower has no cash to pay until maturity and gets a tax deduction for imputed interest. The investor can lock in a high yield and does not have to reinvest the interest. However, the investor has to pay income taxes on a portion of the interest or discount each year, even though no interest is received. Therefore, they are bought by entities such as pension funds, nonprofit organizations, or individual IRAs.

Convertibility

A convertible loan gives the lender the right to convert all or part of a loan into common stock for a stated period at a specified rate of exchange. A warrant is an option to purchase a specific number of shares at a specified price for a stated period. Convertible debt carries a lower interest rate than nonconvertible debt. Warrants do not require the surrender of the debt to obtain the common stock.

Callable Debt

The right to call debt gives the issuer the opportunity to replace high-interest debt with cheaper debt if interest rates decline. The call price is invariably higher than the par value. The difference between the call price and par is referred to as the call premium. The call premium decreases each year until it reaches par value. Because the call provision establishes a limit on the investor's profitability, callable bonds will have a higher yield to maturity than noncallable debt of equal risk.

COVENANTS

Intermediate and long-term lenders generally include a list of conditions in the loan agreement that require the borrower to maintain certain minimum financial levels and ratios and restrict the company's operations. The objective is to enable the lender to call the loan if the borrower's financial condition seriously declines or to limit certain actions that may threaten the recovery of the loan. These conditions are referred to as negative covenants. There is also a list of events that the borrower must execute to protect the company's assets and to timely inform the lender of its financial status. These are referred to as affirmative covenants. Failure to comply with the covenants results in a default and may, if not cured or waived, cause the loan to become immediately due.

Negative covenants may include limitations or restrictions on salaries paid to specified individuals; payment of dividends; additional borrowings; acquisition of fixed assets; loans or advances to affiliates, officers, directors, or shareholders; the sale of assets; the merger with or acquisition of other businesses; and the sale of the existing business. Defaults can also be triggered if certain ratios or amounts fall below specified levels. Maintenance of specified levels of working capital and net worth and financial ratios, such as the debt-to-equity ratio and the current ratio, are usual.

Affirmative covenants usually include agreements to maintain adequate insurance, submit financial information on a timely basis, and to maintain plant and equipment in good condition.

NEGOTIATING TERMS

Drafts of loan agreements should be reviewed by appropriate members of management as well as the company's attorneys and accountants. All conditions agreed to by the lender should be included in the written agreement. Oral assurances are frequently forgotten or are more readily subject to interpretation. Loan proposals should be negotiated with three or four lenders so that a comparison of terms can be made. Market conditions, the financial position, history of operations, and the available collateral will determine the borrower's ability to influence the terms.

Guarantees and Collateral

- If sufficient collateral has been pledged by the business, there should not be a need to pledge personal collateral or give personal guarantees.
- If the business has a history of profitable operations and prompt payments, the need for collateral, either personal or business, or guarantees should be questioned.

- Do not pledge the stock of the borrowing corporation.
- Cross-collateral and cross-guarantees may be excessive.

Covenants

- It is not to the lender's or borrower's advantage to agree to the maintenance of financial levels so close to current levels that an early default is inevitable if there is a temporary drop in operating results shortly after the closing.
- In order to avoid the possibility that newly promulgated accounting principles create defaults, the loan agreement should provide that future calculation of financial requirements be made in conformity with accounting principles in effect at the time of the loan.
- Restrictions on items such as salaries or dividends should allow bonuses or dividends based on a percentage of earnings over a stated amount. This would allow flexibility in compensating key personnel and still protect the lender.
- Limitations on capital expenditures should permit the carryover of unused prior years' annual limits.
- Restrictions on ownership transfers or sales should permit a reasonable level of transfers to family members for estate planning purposes.

Prepayment

A right to prepay is important if interest rates drop or if, for example, loan covenants would prevent management from entering into an opportune merger. Avoid prepayment penalties, if possible.

Interest and Other Costs

Lenders are competitive and, depending on market conditions, rates and costs are negotiable, and a comparison of charges by

different lenders should be made. A summary of potential costs
follows:

1. Interest cost, usually based on the prime rate or on
   LIBOR (London Inter-Bank Offered Rate), plus or minus
   a stated percentage. The rate above or below prime or
   LIBOR reflects market conditions and the borrower's
   creditworthiness.
2. Standby fees on undrawn balances of credit lines or loan
   commitments.
3. Cost of maintaining compensating balances.
4. Cost of audits and special procedures on the collateral
   and on internal controls related to the collateral.
5. If debt is convertible or was sold with warrants to
   purchase stock, the difference between the value of the
   company at the date of conversion or exercise and the
   conversion or exercise price represents an additional cost
   of borrowing.
6. Prepayment penalties on long-term loans.
7. Finder's fees to persons who locate the money.
8. Where receivables are factored, the factor's commissions
   less the savings achieved by the elimination or reduction
   of: (a) the credit and collections department, (b) accounts
   receivable bookkeeping, (c) compensating balances, and
   (d) bad debt losses.

SOURCES OF DEBT FINANCING

A summary of the major sources of debt financing is as follows:

Commercial Banks

- They are short- to intermediate-term (up to five years)
  lenders.
- They generally require collateral or personal guarantees.
- They may require compensating balances.

- Intermediate-term loan agreements will include restrictive covenants.
- They do not lend to start-up companies.

Commercial Finance Companies

- They are intermediate-term lenders (up to five years) that always require collateral, usually accounts receivable, inventories, and plant and equipment.
- They do not require compensating balances.
- Interest rates are higher than those charged by commercial banks because the customers or industries serviced are considered riskier.
- They perform factoring functions.
- Agreements usually contain restrictive covenants.
- Loan guarantees are usually required.

Leasing Companies

- They can vary from very short term to long term (up to life of asset), depending on lessee needs.
- They require low or no initial cash investment.
- The total costs over the life of the lease are usually higher than borrowing.
- The lessor retains title to the asset—no additional collateral is necessary.

Insurance Companies and Pension Funds

- They fund intermediate- and long-term requirements.
- They may be willing to lend to businesses not meeting usual financial standards if warrants or conversion rights to common stock are included.
- Except for mortgages and acquisitions loans, loans do not ordinarily require collateral.
- Restrictive covenants are always included in the loan agreement.
- They usually do not fund start-up companies.

Appendix
SUMMARY OF DEBT AND EQUITY FEATURES

		Equity	
	Debt	*Preferred*	*Common*
Required payments	Yes	No(1)	No(1)
Proceeds included in equity	No	Yes(1)	Yes(1)
Shares in future growth of company	No(2)	No(2)(3)	Yes
Interest on debt or dividends on equity are:			
1. Tax deductible	Yes	No	No
2. Includable in taxable income of holder	Yes	(4)	(4)
Dilution of existing common shareholders' control	No(2)	No(2)(6)	Yes(6)
Preference in liquidation	Yes	(5)	No
Restrictive or negative convenants— failure to meet can lead to a default	Yes	(6)	(6)
Reduces earnings per share of common stock of public companies:			
1. Interest on debt or dividends on equity	Yes	Yes(7)	No
2. Convertible debt or convertible preferred stock	(8)	(8)	N/A

Notes:

(1) Preferred or common stock redeemable at the option of the holder requires repayment. Public companies cannot include stock redeemable at the option of the holder as part of the equity.

(2) Debt or preferred stock that is convertible into common stock will, if the holder converts, share in the company's future growth and dilute control.

(3) Participating preferred holders share with common stock in any dividends above the regular preferred dividend and after a specified level of dividend on common has been declared.

(4) Subject to certain restrictions and limitations, a C corporation may deduct 70 or 80 percent of dividends from unaffiliated domestic corporations and 100 percent of the dividends received from other members of an affiliated group.

(5) In liquidation, preferred stock ranks ahead of common stock and behind debt.

(6) Agreements to privately place equity capital usually contain restrictions and/or allow additional seats on the board of directors if stipulated earnings are not achieved.

(7) Preferred dividends should be deducted to arrive at net earnings or loss applicable to common stock. Unpaid preferred dividends (if the preferred is cumulative), periodic increases in the carrying amount of redeemable preferred, and increases in the carrying amount of increasing rate preferred should also be deducted.

(8) If debt or preferred stock is convertible into common stock and is classified as a common stock equivalent (as defined by accounting rules), it will only affect earnings per share if it reduces primary earnings per share. If convertible securities do not meet the accounting criteria as a common stock equivalent, the fully diluted earnings per share will be affected if the result is a reduction in earnings per share.

Chapter Four

Securities Offerings Exempt from SEC Registration

Rosenman & Colin

ENTREPRENEUR'S OVERVIEW

The federal securities laws regulate the offering and sale of securities to the public. The Securities Act of 1933 requires that, subject to limited exceptions, any public offering or distribution of securities be registered with the Securities and Exchange Commission (the SEC) and be made through the use of a written prospectus containing information required by the SEC.

The prospectus must be filed with the SEC as part of a registration statement before it may be distributed to offerees. The SEC normally reviews the prospectus to ensure that it contains sufficient disclosure of the information the SEC requires before the securities may be sold. The process generally requires the assistance of attorneys and accountants and can be costly and time-consuming.

Securities may be offered and sold without registration and without a formal prospectus, however, if they are not being offered or sold pursuant to a public offering, or if the offering or sale complies with an exemption from registration under the Securities Act. Generally, an offering is not considered to constitute a public offering if limitations are made as to the size of the offering, the number or types of investors who may invest, or other factors relating to the offering.

This chapter will discuss the following offering exemptions from the registration requirement:

- Section 4(2) offerings.
- Regulation D offerings.
- Regulation A offerings.
- Intrastate offerings.
- Offerings of restricted securities to qualified institutional buyers under Rule 144A.

In addition, the chapter will compare exempt offerings to registered offerings. It will also provide an illustration concerning exempt offerings.

This chapter only discusses exemptions from registration under the federal securities laws. It does not address state regulation of securities offerings and sales. Every state and the District of Columbia have regulations that must be considered by any company contemplating a securities offering.

Typically, securities sold pursuant to exempt offerings are subject to resale restrictions. This chapter does not discuss all of the exemptions that may be available to purchasers of securities in exempt offerings who wish to resell such securities.

SECTION 4(2) OFFERINGS

Section 4(2) of the Securities Act exempts from the Securities Act's registration requirement any offering by a company of its own securities, if such offering is not a public offering. This exemption from the registration requirement is relied on more often than any other offering exemption.

Criteria for reliance on the Section 4(2) exemption are found in case law and are not very exact. Generally, the company must consider the number of offerees, the amount and the type of securities being offered, the intent of investors not to redistribute the securities, the manner in which the offering is conducted, and other factors that would cause the company reasonably to believe it is making an isolated offer of securities to offerees who can fend for themselves and that such securities will not be reoffered to the public.

Because the standards for determining if an offering constitutes a valid Section 4(2) offering are not clear-cut, the exemption is generally relied on in situations where a few offerees, typically financial institutions or other sophisticated investors, have already been located and are in a position to negotiate their investment. If the offerees have been located through solicitation of a larger group, however, the solicitation constitutes an offer, and the Section 4(2) exemption may not be available.

There is no specific disclosure requirement or formal resale restrictions for Section 4(2) offerings, although purchasers are to purchase for their own account and not with the intent to resell. Since the antifraud provisions of the Securities Act apply, notwithstanding the Section 4(2) exemption, some form of disclosure documentation is usually furnished to offerees. General advertisement or solicitation is clearly inappropriate.

REGULATION D OFFERINGS

The SEC has adopted Regulation D under the Securities Act to set forth criteria for limited offerings that, if satisfied, will ensure that such offerings will not be considered by the SEC to constitute a public offering and thus will not require registration with the SEC. Unlike a Section 4(2) offering, a company making a Regulation D offering does not need to limit the number of offerees.

Regulation D offerings are limited, however, in either aggregate dollar amount, which can be raised through such offering, or the number and status of the potential purchasers, or both.

Regulation D imposes certain requirements as to information to be provided to the potential purchasers, depending on the size of the offering and the types of potential purchasers to whom it is made. The required information is generally as extensive as that required in a prospectus for a registered offering but does not need to be submitted to the SEC for review or approval.

The manner in which securities may be sold under Regulation D is also restricted; advertisement and general solicitation are prohibited unless the aggregate offering price does not exceed $1 million and the company is allowed to use the $1 million or less Regulation D offering exemption described below.

Securities purchased in a Regulation D offering are subject to resale restrictions unless the aggregate offering price does not exceed $1 million and the company is allowed to use the $1 million or less Regulation D offering exemption described below.

Restrictions on Regulation D Offerings

Regulation D offerings are broken into three categories. They are as follows:

- Offerings of securities for an aggregate dollar amount not exceeding $1 million made by companies that are not investment companies, development-stage companies lacking specific business plans, or companies subject to periodic reporting requirements under the Securities Exchange Act of 1934.
- Offerings of securities for an aggregate dollar amount not exceeding $5 million made by companies other than investment companies.
- Offerings of securities for an aggregate dollar amount of more than $5 million.

There is no disclosure requirement or resale restriction for offerings of $1 million or less, nor is the number or status of the purchasers for such offerings or the manner in which they may be contacted limited. In larger offerings, specific disclosure is required to be made to investors, and sales may only be made to investors who are "accredited investors," as defined in Regulation D, and up to an additional 35 investors who do not satisfy the definition of accredited investor. There is no restriction on the number or types of offerees; the restrictions only apply to actual purchasers.

An accredited investor is an entity or an individual viewed by the SEC as not needing the protection provided by the detailed disclosure required in a prospectus. Regulation D's definition of an accredited investor includes any bank or other specified financial institution, any insurance company, any trust or ERISA plan with total assets in excess of $5 million, any broker-dealer in securities, and any individual having annual earnings for at least two years, and projected for the current year, in excess of

$200,000 (or $300,000 jointly with a spouse), or having a net worth (or joint net worth with a spouse) in excess of $1 million.

If the aggregate offering price does not exceed $5 million, the company making the offering need not inquire about the knowledge or sophistication of the investors, other than to ensure that sales are not made to more than 35 investors who are not accredited investors (assuming the aggregate offering price exceeds $1 million). If the aggregate offering price exceeds $5 million, the company must ascertain that each investor is either an accredited investor or, either alone or with his adviser, has such knowledge and experience in financial and business matters that he is capable of evaluating the merits and risks of the prospective investment. Typically, the company will fulfill this obligation by requiring each potential purchaser to complete an investor questionnaire that contains questions concerning his or her business and investment experience and his or her ability to assume an investment risk.

The total offering price for all securities sold within 12 months prior to the commencement of any Regulation D offering in reliance upon any exemption from the Securities Act registration requirements must be added to the aggregate offering prices for the contemplated Regulation D offering for the purpose of determining under which Regulation D category an offering is to be considered. Thus, if a Regulation D offering of only $500,000 is to be made, but the company sold over $500,000 in securities pursuant to exempt offerings within the preceding year, the Regulation D offering would be considered to be in excess of $1 million, and disclosure and investor requirements, as well as resale and advertisement restrictions, would need to be satisfied.

In addition, if similar offerings or sales of securities by the company have been or will be made within a six-month period prior to the start or following the completion of a Regulation D offering, they may be combined with the contemplated Regulation D offering to calculate both the number of purchasers and the aggregate dollar amount being offered for purposes of determining compliance with Regulation D. In determining whether to consider such prior or future offers or sales, the SEC looks to see if they are part of a single plan of financing, if they involve the same class of securities, if sales are made at or about the same time, if the securities are sold for the same type of consideration, and if securities are being sold for the same general purpose.

Disclosure Requirements under Regulation D

As noted above, Regulation D does not require any information to be provided to potential investors in an offering not exceeding $1 million. In larger offerings, disclosures of specified information are required to be made to those investors who are not accredited investors.

In such cases, companies that are not currently subject to SEC reporting requirements (usually because they have not made any registered offerings) must prepare a private placement memorandum containing all information that could be important to understand the company, its business, and the securities being offered. The memorandum must be delivered to each potential investor, other than accredited investors, within a reasonable time prior to any purchase by such potential investor.

The memorandum must include the same type of information as required in a prospectus or, if the company could conduct the offering pursuant to Regulation A (discussed further in this chapter), the same type of information as required in a Regulation A offering circular.

The memorandum must contain fairly detailed financial information, the extent of which varies with the size of the offering. If the aggregate offering price is less than $2 million, only the company's balance sheet needs to be audited; otherwise, all of the financial statements must be audited unless the company can demonstrate that obtaining audited financial statements would involve unreasonable effort or expense.

While the disclosure requirements for larger offerings may become as onerous as those for a registered offering, the private placement memorandum, with limited exception, is not required to be filed with the SEC.

Advertisement

General solicitation or advertisement is prohibited in a Regulation D offering of over $1 million. This prohibition enjoins any advertisement, article, notice, or other communication published in any newspaper or magazine or broadcast over television or radio, or any seminar if the persons in attendance were invited by any of the foregoing means. Brokers and dealers may not generally solicit their clients with respect to the Regulation D offering unless the clients have shown an interest and ability to invest in offerings of such nature.

Resale Restrictions

Securities purchased pursuant to a Regulation D offering of over $1 million may not be resold unless they are registered or an exemption from the registration requirement is available. Upon any sale pursuant to Regulation D, the company must make clear to the purchaser, and must indicate in writing on any certificate evidencing the securities sold, that the securities are subject to resale restrictions.

Postoffering Requirements

Within 15 days after the first sale pursuant to a Regulation D offering, the company must file a notice of sale with the SEC. Such a notice is not subject to SEC review or approval but does alert the SEC to the offering and may lead the SEC to investigate to see if the offering, in fact, complies with Regulation D. Such investigation is uncommon.

REGULATION A OFFERINGS

Offerings that comply with the provisions of Regulation A, adopted by the SEC, are exempt from registration under the Securities Act. The aggregate offering price may not exceed $5 million. In this respect, Regulation A is an alternative to a small Regulation D offering. The number and type of investors are not restricted. Certain disclosure must be made to potential investors, however, in an offering circular that must be filed with the SEC as part of an offering statement.

The SEC may review the offering circular and require it to be revised before sales can occur. Review is less likely, however, than if the offering were a registered offering, and the requirements for the offering circular are less onerous than prospectus requirements.

Restrictions on Regulation A Offerings

The exemption provided by Regulation A may only be utilized by private companies that are not subject to SEC reporting requirements. Development-stage companies lacking specific business plans; investment companies; and companies offering certain interests in oil, gas, or other mineral rights may not use Regulation A.

Unlike Regulation D offerings, which may only be made by companies selling their own securities, security holders may engage or participate in Regulation A offerings to sell their interests, but only if the company has had net income from continuing operations in at least one of its last two fiscal years.

The aggregate dollar price for the securities being offered (including those offered by security holders) may not exceed $5 million less the total dollar amount of all securities sold by the company or any security holders pursuant to other Regulation A offerings within the 12 months prior to the commencement of the current offering. The total purchase price of securities being offered by security holders may not exceed $1.5 million.

Disclosure Requirements under Regulation A

A preliminary offering circular containing information prescribed by the SEC must be filed with the SEC (at its main office in Washington, DC, or an appropriate regional office) before the Regulation A offering is commenced. The preliminary offering circular may omit pricing information. Unless the SEC elects to review the offering circular and delay its effectiveness, it becomes effective 20 days after filing. At such time, the company should include pricing information, and the offering circular is considered final.

A sale may not be made unless the preliminary or final offering circular is delivered to the potential purchaser two days in advance of confirmation of the sale and the final offering circular is delivered to the purchaser upon sale confirmation.

The offering circular must contain information concerning factors that may make a potential investment in the company risky, information about the company's business and properties, information about the planned use of proceeds from the offering and about the company's capitalization and dividend history, information concerning the company's management and its compensation and the company's major stockholders, and the company's analysis of its financial condition and results of operations.

A balance sheet and income statements for the past two years and an interim statement covering the period from the end of the prior fiscal year to the end of the most recent fiscal quarter must be furnished. They do not need to be audited, unless audited statements are available.

Advertisement

Advertisement of securities offered in a Regulation A offering is permitted but in limited form. Written or broadcast solicitations of interest are permitted prior to the filing of the preliminary offering circular, subject to certain limitations and only if the text is first filed with the SEC (a process known as "testing the waters"), and offers and sales may not be made until the offering circular is furnished to investors as described above. After the offering circular is effective, the contents of permitted advertisements are not limited as long as the statements contained in the advertisement are not false or misleading, but the text must be filed with the SEC.

Resale Restrictions

Securities purchased pursuant to a Regulation A offering are not subject to resale restrictions.

Postoffering Requirements

The seller(s) must report to the SEC on sales of securities under a Regulation A offering, and on the use of the proceeds, every six months until the completion or termination of the offering and the final application of proceeds.

INTRASTATE OFFERINGS

The Securities Act only regulates the offer and sale of securities in interstate commerce and leaves to each state the regulation of the offer and sale of securities made solely within such state. Thus, intrastate offerings, or offerings and sales that satisfy the SEC's regulations as occurring solely within one state, need not be registered.

Restrictions on Intrastate Offerings

The SEC strictly defines intrastate offerings. The issuer must be incorporated and have its principal office within one state. Eighty percent of its gross revenues and assets must be derived from and located within such state, and it must intend to use 80 percent of the offering proceeds to operate within such state.

The company offering and selling the securities and the purchasers and offerees must all have their principal residences within the state. The company must obtain written confirmation of residence from each purchaser in the intrastate offering. One offeree or purchaser who resides out of state will destroy the exemption for all of the securities offered.

These are very onerous requirements, and it is believed that relatively few financings can satisfy the exemption.

Any other offering of similar securities, or securities sold for the same general purpose or consideration, within six months before or after the intrastate offering must also satisfy the intrastate offering requirements with respect to the same state in which the contemplated offering is to be made.

The SEC has stated that only the company whose securities are being offered may rely on the exemption; selling security holders may not. Judicial decisions have held, however, that controlling stockholders may sell their holdings in exempt intrastate offerings although they are not technically included in the SEC rule governing the exemption.

Both companies and controlling stockholders must, of course, comply with the registration and other requirements of the state in which the offering is to be conducted.

Resale Restrictions

The securities must "come to rest" within the state of issuance. This means that, for a period of nine months from the last sale in the intrastate offering, none of the securities offered pursuant to the intrastate exemption can be resold to purchasers who do not have their primary homes within the same state in which the offering was made. The security certificates must state this resale restriction, and companies usually obtain written agreement from purchasers to this restriction.

RESTRICTED SECURITIES SALES TO QUALIFIED INSTITUTIONAL BUYERS

As noted above, securities purchased in Regulation D offerings may not be offered for resale or resold unless they are registered or an exemption from registration for such resale is available. Such an exemption exists under the SEC's Rule 144A if the securities are offered and sold only to financial institutions that satisfy the SEC's definition of "qualified institutional buyer" or QIB. The QIB exemption from registration is only available for the resale of securities: a company may not rely on it to sell its own securities. A separate exemption must be found for the primary offering.

Restrictions on QIB Offerings

Generally, a QIB is a specified type of institution with a minimum of $100 million in investment securities, other than securities issued by that institution or its affiliates. The types of institutions that can be QIBs are typically the same types of institutions that come within the definition of accredited investor for purposes of Regulation D. For banks and savings and loan associations to qualify as QIBs, they must also have an audited net worth of at least $25 million. The investment volume requirement is less for securities dealers to qualify as QIBs.

The seller must make reasonable inquiry to be sure that each offeree and purchaser is a QIB. Such inquiry may consist of reviewing publicly available information or obtaining written certifications from the offeree's officers.

Securities may not be sold under the QIB exemption if they are of the same class as securities listed on a national securities exchange or quoted in a national automated interdealer quotation system such as NASDAQ. The purpose of this restriction is to prevent affiliates of a company from creating a second private market for the company's securities when such securities are traded in a public market.

Disclosure Requirements

Although the company is not the seller in a QIB offering, the company (unless it files periodic reports with the SEC) is required to provide to the holder and the prospective purchaser, upon request, a brief description of the company's business, the products and services it offers, and a recent balance sheet and profit and loss and retained earnings statements for the preceding two years. The financial statements should be audited, if audited statements are reasonably available.

Resale Restrictions

Securities purchased by QIBs pursuant to the exemption described above may not be reoffered or resold except to other QIBs, unless they are registered or an exemption from registration for the reoffering or resale is available. Sellers must ensure that purchasers are aware of this restriction.

COMPARISON OF EXEMPT OFFERINGS TO REGISTERED OFFERINGS

The registration process, which will be discussed in detail in Chapter Five, is generally more time-consuming and expensive than conducting an exempt offering. If securities are to be registered, a formal prospectus must be prepared that will disclose business, operating, and financial information about the company in detail. Lawyers, accountants, and other professionals are needed to draft and produce the prospectus, which must be filed with the SEC and may be subject to its review. Once effective, without or following SEC review, as the SEC chooses, the prospectus must be distributed to all offerees. It can create liability for all parties that helped produce it should the information disclosed be found to be false or misleading.

Registration, however, allows a company to offer an unlimited dollar amount of securities without any restrictions as to offerees or purchasers of the securities. Registered securities may be easier to sell because resale of such securities is not restricted.

On the other hand, companies generally are able to arrange an offering more quickly and less expensively under the exemptions described in this chapter than by going through the registration process. In general, fewer documents need to be created and distributed, reducing the work for lawyers and accountants. Further, a less complicated and time-consuming offering process will use less of the company's human resources that could be otherwise utilized to benefit the company.

Should the company elect to have an exempt offering, however, it must be able to comply with the restrictions governing the exemption for the duration of the offering and, perhaps, some time thereafter. These restrictions consist generally of limitations on the aggregate dollar amount of securities sold (including sales before and after the offering), limitations on who can be offered the securities, limitations on advertising and distributing information, and limitations on resales.

Appendix
CHOOSING AMONGST ALTERNATIVES

Kid's Korner, Inc., a company organized under the laws of California (the "Company"), is engaged in the business of producing and selling children's toys. It has been quite successful despite its short duration, having had positive net earnings during each of its past two fiscal years in excess of $500,000. It has $2 million in debt and is owned by the Lambert family.

The Lamberts actively run the company. They have decided that they would like to sell stock in the company to raise funds to pay off some of its debt and serve as working capital. They would also like to receive some of the proceeds as a return on their initial $25,000 investment. They do not want to relinquish control of the company, however.

They are reluctant to conduct a registered offering if an exemption can be found. They do not want the company to undergo the time and expense to prepare a prospectus and face possible SEC review. They also do not want to have to comply with the continuing SEC reporting and other requirements imposed on public companies. They do not care if the stock to be sold is subject to resale restrictions as long as purchasers can be found who will buy restricted securities.

The Lamberts first considered a Section 4(2) offering. They did not know of any institutional investors interested in investing in the company, however, and wanted to be able to offer stock to more than a handful of potential investors. They preferred relying on an exemption that would not limit the number of offerees.

The Lamberts then considered a Regulation D offering. They had heard a fair amount about private placements and had thought the company could handle a small one. The company would offer less than $1 million of common stock so it would not need to distribute any particular required form of information and would not need to inquire about the investment sophistication of its purchasers.

The Lamberts concluded, however, that a Regulation D offering might not serve their needs. There was no apparent market for the company's stock, and Regulation D would limit their ability to advertise. Interested investors, should any be found, would probably ask for a private placement memorandum or brochure to describe the company and the offering. Moreover, resale restrictions could make the company's stock impossible to sell if potential purchasers thought they would not be able to re-market the stock, especially as QIBs may not be interested in

businesses as small as the company's. Finally, the Lamberts realized that they would not be able to sell their own stock as part
of the Regulation D offering, so they would not be able to realize
any return personally.

They next considered an intrastate offering. There would be
little federal regulation and no restriction on the size of the offering. The problems of needing a sales brochure and creating a
market remained, however. Furthermore, while states generally
have small offering exemptions, California's exemption would
limit the number of offerees as well as purchasers, and its registration process could be quite onerous. Moreover, the company
was located near the Oregon border and hoped to make sales in
that state.

The Lamberts then considered a Regulation A offering. The
total offering price could not exceed $5 million, but the Lamberts
did not expect to raise that much through sale of a minority interest. An offering circular would have to be prepared but could
serve as the company's main sales material. While it would have
to be filed with the SEC at least 20 days prior to the proposed
offering, it could be filed in the SEC's Los Angeles office (rather
than its Washington, DC, office), it may not even be reviewed by
the SEC, and the company could make limited advertisements in
the meantime. The stock sold in the Regulation A offering could
be sold to anyone, and purchasers could resell without restriction. The Lamberts could also sell some of their stock in the
offering.

Regulation D offerings may be better for other companies that
are less concerned about size and investor restrictions than about
the time and cost of preparing a Regulation A offering circular.
Typically, this is the case if the offering is intended for accredited
investors or very few other investors. Intrastate offerings are best
for truly local companies that can raise funds in their own state,
especially if such state's securities regulations are not too onerous. Section 4(2) offerings are appropriate if a small number of
sophisticated investors have already been located who are interested in investing.

Each company needs to consider its own potential investor
base, capital needs, time and expense constraints, and other relevant factors in determining which type of offering to make.

Chapter Five

Going Public

Bear Stearns & Co., Inc.

ENTREPRENEUR'S OVERVIEW

An initial public offering (IPO) is a milestone in the life of a company and a symbol of corporate success. In going public, you are giving others a chance to buy a piece of your business and to share in its profitability. Most successful IPOs involve companies with experienced and committed management that is able to demonstrate a solid business history with proven products, significant assets, strong earnings, and a potential for further growth. In some industries (e.g., biotechnology), start-up concerns can raise money in the capital markets. These cases are the exception and generally feature a breakthrough product or technology. Like any business venture, however, a public offering must be carefully planned. Your knowledge of the intricacies of the public offering process will enable you to anticipate problems before they occur and to allocate your time and resources efficiently.

This chapter will help you determine whether an initial public offering will suit your overall business strategy. We will discuss the major advantages and disadvantages of going public and the professionals whose assistance you will need. We will also explain the key steps in the underwriting process. By the time you finish this chapter, you should have a clear overview of what is involved in taking your company public.

THE PROS AND CONS OF AN IPO

Advantages of Going Public

- Raising capital: When the growth of a company can no longer be financed by retained earnings or debt financing, an IPO is often the best means for raising the money you need to accomplish your business objectives. The public markets (also called the capital markets) are often your best source of money because the shares of a publicly traded company are more valuable than the shares of a private company. The reason for this lies in the liquidity provided by the capital markets. The fact that shares can be sold at any time increases their value.

- Liquidity for the original shareholders: The liquidity of a publicly traded stock also benefits the original shareholders because their stakes in the company are now more readily marketable. However, officers, directors, and major shareholders are subject to restrictions before they can sell their stock in the public market without registration (Rule 144 of 1933 Act). The restrictions include a holding period and limitations on the amount of securities that may be sold during a given period. Sometimes, if feasible, both the company and shareholders sell stock in an IPO to meet the needs of major shareholders who wish to cash in on a portion of their holdings and diversify their personal investments.

- Estate planning: A public company will also make estate planning simpler for the family of an entrepreneur. If estate taxes are owed, the family can sell stock to cover the tax liability. On the other hand, the valuation for estate tax purposes is usually higher for a company when it is public.

- Currency for the future: The stock of a public company can also be used to finance future acquisitions. When the business strategy of a company includes plans for diversification, geographic expansion, or other strategic ventures, the need for capital becomes a primary concern. An IPO can be a useful source of currency to fund these projects.

- Company profile: Once you become a public company, investors will want to know as much about you as they can.

This often leads to a heightened profile for your company and its products. The increase in visibility may, in turn, lead to additional business opportunities.

- Incentive-based compensation for employees: A company with publicly traded stock has a powerful tool to attract and retain quality personnel. Employees with an equity stake in the company have a strong incentive to make decisions that are in the best short- and long-term interests of the company.
- Increased opportunities for additional financing: The IPO may be just the beginning of your company's relationship with the capital markets. If your company story is marketed well and investors are receptive, you will be able to raise additional capital with greater ease at a later date. This may be done with another stock offering, or a debt or convertible stock offering. The type of securities issued will depend on the cost of capital at that time. Your investment bankers will advise you on this issue.

Disadvantages of Going Public

- Time requirements: The process of bringing a company public will demand a great deal of your time. You will need to meet regularly with bankers, lawyers, and accountants and will be responsible for organizing a great deal of financial material. Finally, you will be called upon to help sell your deal to the investment community. A typical IPO takes four months.
- Cost: An IPO is expensive. It will cost 8 percent to 10 percent of the total amount raised in the offering. A commission, or "gross spread" is paid to the investment banks. The amount of the "spread" will be negotiated but will be 7 percent to 9 percent of the offering. The gross spread is comprised of the management fee (20 percent), which is paid to the lead managing investment bank; the underwriting fee (20 percent), which is also paid to the lead manager for putting its own capital at risk; and the selling commission (60 percent), which is paid to salespeople. In addition to the gross spread,

an IPO involves out-of-pocket expenses for the company. For example, a $10 million common stock IPO normally runs between $200,000 and $500,000 in out-of-pocket expenses. Legal, accounting, and printing can vary depending on the complexity of issues, delays for market, or other reasons and the resulting multiple filings.

- Financial disclosure: Selling shares to the public creates the responsibility of sharing information with investors. All material details, including important trade relationships, must now be disclosed. Additionally, you will be required to file quarterly and annual reports with the SEC.

- Control issues: If a majority of your company is sold to the public, you will no longer have a controlling interest in its operation. Ownership dilution will increase as a result of any subsequent equity offerings, acquisitions of other companies for stock and option, and warrant exercises. On the other hand, effective control can often be maintained in a public company with less than majority ownership, especially if the public ownership is widespread. Further, private placements or loan agreements may, in fact, also cause a loss of control by imposing certain restrictions. These restrictions may include limits on salaries and dividends, the right to approve expansion into new geographic areas or new lines of business, and the right to nominate a majority of the board of directors should the enterprise be unprofitable for a specific number of years.

- Investor pressure for short-term results: Because you will be filing quarterly, investors will be evaluating your performance at least once every three months. Investor sensitivity to earnings momentum can result in stock price volatility and intensify pressure to show short-term profitability, possibly at the expense of long-term goals.

- Unsuccessful offering: There is the risk that the IPO will not be successful. Expenditures for legal, accounting, printing, and the underwriters' expense allowance can be quite significant at the point the offering is abandoned. Some companies obtain funds through a private placement prior to the IPO in order to finance the expenses of the IPO. The cost of a private placement adds to the price of an abandoned IPO. In addition, a lot of time and energy will have been spent on the IPO by management.

- Recurring costs: There are additional expenses for a publicly owned company. Recurring expenses include legal, accounting, and printing costs for the preparation, filing, and distributing of proxy material and annual reports to shareholders and the fees for a transfer agent, a registrar, and a public relations consultant.

GETTING YOUR HOUSE IN ORDER

If, after weighing the pros and cons of going public, you determine that an IPO is an appropriate financial vehicle for your company, you will need to begin to organize the data used by the underwriters throughout the IPO process.

Financial

There may be an absence of the required number of years of audited financial statements for the issuer (three years for an S-1 or two years for an SB-2; see later discussion) or for significant business acquisitions (one to three years—see Chapter Eight). Discuss with the auditors whether the unaudited years can be audited currently. There may be an inability to retroactively audit the necessary financials. It is best to find out before much cost and energy are expended.

Review complex and significant accounting transactions of the past three to five years to better assure that the accounting treatment was substantively correct. Aggressive tax positions should be reconsidered with a view to settling likely contingencies before going public.

Legal

You should take time to review your company's legal structure with corporate counsel. You must determine whether your current corporate structure should be changed because it precludes a public offering (e.g., several corporations each owned directly by stockholders). Some of the basic legal questions involve issues of shareholder approval that may be required for changes in ownership, or the existence of shareholder or control agreements. These are issues that you can discuss with your corporate counsel prior to beginning the underwriting process.

The board of directors will have the responsibility for setting overall policy for the company. A publicly traded company is generally required to have at least two outside directors on its board. It is a good idea to choose individuals who know your industry well and are strong in areas where your company is not. A board with a number of strong independent directors will give the company added credibility with investors.

It is advisable to appoint a point person, an individual who will be responsible for seeing that all of the necessary deadlines are met. This person should be familiar with the information being compiled so if there is a problem he or she will be able to get to work on the solution immediately. Much of the information needed by the bankers and lawyers is cumulative. A delay in gathering one portion will affect the whole process.

SELECTING THE PROFESSIONALS TO HELP YOU

Selecting the Lawyers

Your lawyers will be heavily involved in the disclosure aspects of the offering. They will have primary operational responsibility for insuring that your offering complies with federal securities laws. In addition, your lawyers will be involved in many of the discussions held between your company and the investment bank. In-house counsel is likely to be unfamiliar with many of the issues that arise in a public offering. Therefore, it is advisable to retain experienced outside counsel for the IPO process. Look for counsel with extensive securities experience.

Selecting the Auditors

In addition to auditing the company's financial statements, auditors advise management on the impact of a public offering on the company, suggest alternative financing vehicles, and study the tax consequences of being a public company. Once a company decides to make a public offering, the accountants audit and issue an opinion on the financial statements and issue a comfort letter to the underwriters. Auditors also participate actively in the review and critique of the filing and disclosure documents. They assist the company in preparing responses to regulatory comments and, in some cases, take the lead in discussing these documents with the SEC accounting staff.

In choosing an accountant, look for experience with the SEC and with the IPO process, and reputation. Meet the partner who will be in charge of your engagement and ascertain the extent of his or her personal involvement. The relationship with your accountants typically extends well beyond the IPO process, as they continue to advise, audit, and oversee the completion of the disclosure forms required by the SEC.

Selecting the Underwriter(s)

The selection of an underwriter (also called an investment banker) is one of the most important decisions you will make as you prepare to go public. The investment bank you choose will manage the entire underwriting, which means the bank will be responsible for analyzing your company and coordinating the sale and distribution of stock at the conclusion of the deal. The following criteria will be helpful in selecting a banker:

- Expertise: An experienced investment banker will have a keen sense of what will sell in the marketplace, an instinct for determining the best timing for a deal, and the ability to place stock with investors when the deal is completed. Your banker should be, or have the ability to become, an expert in your business and industry.
- Reputation: The reputation of the investment banker is important because investors will associate your stock with the bank that is coordinating the deal. When electing a bank, look for a track record comprised of offerings for companies of your size and in your industry group. Investment banks have areas of specialization. Strength in one area does not necessary indicate strength in another.
- Distribution: The ability to distribute stock to a diverse client base is a key component of an investment bank's job.

Stocks are sold to individuals (retail sales) and to institutions, such as pension or mutual funds (institutional sales). Your investment bank should be able to demonstrate the ability to place stock with both types of investors.

• Research support: Once your stock begins to trade on an exchange, it is important that investors know about your company. Your investment bank should have a respected analyst who covers your industry. Check with institutional investors to see how they rate the bank's analyst. The financial press regularly publishes lists of "all-star" analysts.

• Aftermarket trading support: The firm's trading capabilities and its willingness to take positions in your stock are crucial to the success of your IPO. New issues are subject to volatility following their offering. An investment bank will make an effort to buy and sell stock in the marketplace in order to stabilize the issue. A good investment bank will place both its capital and reputation behind your deal.

Letter of Intent

After selecting the underwriter, the company will be asked to sign a letter of intent. The letter of intent will indicate that it is merely a statement of intent and not a legally binding agreement, except for the company's obligations to pay for certain expenses whether or not the offering is completed. The letter of intent will usually include terms such as the expected number of shares to be sold, the expected offering price, the underwriter's overallotment option, the requirement for a cold comfort letter from the independent accountants, whether the offering will be underwritten on a firm commitment or a best-efforts basis, warrants issuable to the underwriter, the underwriter's preferential rights on future financings, the underwriter's discount or commissions, and responsibility for expenses.

Selecting the Registrar and Transfer Agent

The registrar is retained by the company to issue certificates to the new shareholders. The transfer agent maintains the shareholders' ledger cards, recording the transfer of shares from one person to another. Work with your bankers to select a registrar and transfer agent.

THE IPO PROCESS

An IPO requires teamwork between management, the accountants, the lawyers, and the investment bankers. All work together on three major tasks: (1) analyzing the company to determine where it should be valued in relation to other similar companies in its industry; (2) registering the offering with the SEC; and (3) marketing the offering to investors. This work is accomplished in four phases as outlined in Appendix B at the end of this chapter. A more detailed discussion of the process follows.

Analyzing the Company

Valuation. Prior to an IPO, an investment bank will analyze a company in order to estimate its value in the public market. While the bankers follow a rigorous procedure in an attempt to factor in all relevant issues, the market sets the actual price for every security. Valuation is more of an art than a science.

Typically, the investment bank examines the entire financial makeup of the company. Not merely the magnitude, but the quality of earnings is assessed. The ratio of debt to equity, earnings as percentage of sales, earnings as percentage of assets, profit margins, operating margins, gross returns, leverage (amount and type of debt), growth potential, and the overall quality of the balance sheet are scrutinized. Less tangible elements of a company's structure are also weighed. These include, for example, the quality of the management, the diversity and depth of the product line, the quality of operations, and the nature of the customer base. Next, the company is compared to, and contrasted with, other similar publicly traded companies (called comparables). With the comparables used as a benchmark, the bankers determine a rationally based estimate for the value (or capitalization) the company can expect to receive in the marketplace. Almost all IPOs are priced at a discount to their comparables (called a haircut), which reflects the fact that they do not yet have an established performance track record as a public security. This discount is generally 10 percent to 15 percent of their market valuation.

Once management has an idea of their company's estimated market capitalization, they must decide how much of the company they want to sell. Management must balance the company's need for capital with the amount of control they are willing to give up; the larger the percentage of the company sold, the greater the amount of cash raised in the IPO. The trade-off here is unique to every transaction. However, management must sell a sufficient portion of the company in order to provide investors with trading liquidity.

The last step in the valuation process is to determine the actual number of shares to be sold in the IPO. Since the company's total value has already been estimated, the number of shares to be issued is guided primarily by the ratio of smaller retail versus larger institutional participation. The larger the number of shares issued, the smaller the resulting price of each share. Small investors prefer an offering with a large number of shares that trade at a low price per share because it makes it possible to buy and sell small dollar values of stock in each transaction. In addition, transaction costs are reduced because it takes fewer dollars to trade a round lot (100 shares equal one round lot). Institutional investors tend to favor larger per share prices that allow them to move significant amounts of capital without raising or lowering the price of the stock on the exchange. The final decision as to how many shares will be offered will be made based upon the type of investor most likely to buy the issue.

Due diligence.   At the same time the investment bankers are valuing the company, they also perform a due diligence examination. Due diligence is the exhaustive process of insuring the accuracy and completeness of all information about the company. The directors and, to a lesser extent, the bankers, lawyers, and accountants are subject to liability if this is not done. In order to protect investors, the SEC requires that a company disclose all important information prior to selling its stock to the public.

Registration with the SEC

Filing the registration statement.   The SEC is vested with the responsibility of insuring that any company making a public offering fully discloses all important financial information to investors. To accomplish this goal, the SEC has created the registration process.

To register, a company submits its financial biography to the SEC on one of a series of forms, such as the S-1 or SB-2. The information contained in the selected form comprises the registration statement, a portion of which, in its final form, becomes the prospectus.

The registration statement contains information such as a summary of the business, a discussion and analysis by management about the company, a section on the risks associated with this particular issue, and a description of key members of the management team. It is drafted by the company, the managing underwriter, and the attorneys for both the company and underwriter.

The SEC reviews the information submitted on the appropriate form to insure that all material information is properly disclosed. The SEC does not evaluate the investment merits or risks associated with the proposed new issue. After reviewing, the SEC will either approve the registration statement, or ask the company to clarify or augment certain pieces of information. In most cases, the SEC will ask for clarification on some portion of the document. A typical review by the SEC takes approximately one month.

In addition to the federal securities laws, there are the state securities laws commonly referred to as Blue Sky laws. While the federal rules focus only upon the disclosure of information, some states add a fairness or merit requirement. These states look at the offering's fee structure and possible undue benefit by company insiders. The attorneys are responsible for "blue skying" the deal so it can be sold in different states.

The quiet period. In addition to insuring the complete disclosure of information, the SEC controls what is said by a company while it is in the process of issuing stock. From the time a company and its banker agree to issue stock until 90 days after the offering is completed, the company is prohibited from attempting to generate interest in its stock. The company is said to be in the "quiet period."

Events that are regularly reported by the company, such as the introduction of new products or regular advertisements, are permitted. However, public statements that are not normally made as a part of day-to-day operations may be problematic. The company is permitted to announce that it will be issuing stock, but must limit the contents of its remarks to the offering size, timing, and type. Once the registration statement has been filed, the company is not permitted to publish any new sales literature. It is advisable for the company to check with its counsel before making any public statements during the quiet period.

In order to distribute information to prospective investors, the company is permitted to use a draft copy of the registration statement (preliminary prospectus), which has already been submitted to the SEC. This draft copy is called a "red herring" because the cover of the document contains a red-lettered statement emphasizing that the document is only a "draft." The red herring does not contain the date the offering will be made nor the price at which it will be offered.

Marketing and Selling the Deal

The road show. While the company is waiting for final approval from the SEC, the investment bankers organize the road show, which is an informational tour designed to publicize the upcoming offering with professional money managers. The road show is important for both buyers and sellers because it provides a forum for each side to gather information. Buyers are interested in knowing more about the company, and sellers want to gauge the level of interest among prospective buyers.

Syndication. After the registration statement is filed with the SEC, the banker will organize a group of other investment banks to coordinate the distribution of stock to the investment community. This group is called the syndicate. Each member of the syndicate will be responsible for selling a certain amount of stock. During the waiting period, the lead manager will be in contact with the other syndicate members to see how much interest there is in the marketplace for the offering. If market sentiment changes during this period, the offering price is adjusted accordingly.

Pricing the stock.   While the analysis that serves as the basis for a stock's valuation is performed at the beginning of the IPO process, the actual pricing of the stock occurs just after the registration statement is approved by the SEC. The price is based upon the initial valuation and the interest in the marketplace. During the road show, your banker will have had a good opportunity to gauge this interest.

The underwriting agreement.   The underwriting agreement is drawn up between the issuing company and its investment banker on the day before stock is sold to the public. Both parties agree on the offering price of the stock and the commissions, discounts, and other expenses incurred during the underwriting process. In addition, the parties carefully lay out what their responsibilities have been in the offering process and what they will continue to do from this point in time onward. Typically, the company agrees to inform the SEC of any material changes in its operations. It also confirms the accuracy of all information contained in the registration documents. Finally, the company agrees to indemnify the underwriter for errors it may have made in the presentation of financial information. This is an important item because the federal securities laws provide investors with the right to sue for losses sustained because of incorrect, misleading, or omitted material information. After the underwriting agreement is signed, the SEC is notified of the offering price and the registration statement becomes effective.

Aftermarket trading.   Trading begins when the deal is priced on the day after the registration statement becomes effective. The lead manager of the underwriting allocates the stock among syndicate members who, in turn, sell it to their individual clients. The allocation and initial stock sales are made based upon indications of interest given to the salespeople after investors have read the "red herring" and attended the road show.

The first few days of trading are important for any IPO because investors are very sensitive to the way the stock trades in relation to its initial opening price. The lead managers play an important role, at this point, by attempting to ensure price stability for the new issue by making open market purchases and sales. Traders from the lead managing bank will be ready to enter the market to buy the stock if its price drops below the initial offering price. In addition, they will stabilize the stock by selling shares (called green shoe) that were not part of the official offering. This procedure is called "stabilization." (The term *green shoe* is taken from the name of the first company to use this technique.)

When an issue is stabilized, traders increase the supply of stock in the market by selling shares they do not yet own. In effect, they create a short position in the stock. These shares will be repurchased as short-term investors sell their position. If additional shares are needed to cover the bank's short position, the green shoe allows the bank to purchase these shares directly from the company. The amount of stock sold in this manner is limited to 15 percent of the offering. The decision to green shoe must be disclosed prior to the start of trading and must be displayed on the front cover of the preliminary and final prospectus.

The closing.   Five business days after the stock is priced, the underwriter and the issuer exchange cash for stock. The accounting firm will produce a final comfort letter, the bulk of which contains negative assurances concerning unaudited data appearing in the registration statement.

Once the company receives the proceeds of the offering, they are required to file Form SR with the SEC. This form details how the proceeds are to be used by the company. If there are any differences between the use of proceeds section in the prospectus and the actual way the money was spent, the company must justify this to the SEC. Form SR is due within 10 days from the end of the quiet period and must be updated every six months until all of the proceeds are used.

REGISTRATION FORMS SB-1, SB-2, AND S-1

Form S-1 is the form used if no other registration statement form is applicable. The S-1 has been the principal form used in initial public offerings. In 1992, the SEC adopted regulation S-B, a system of new rules and forms designed to give smaller companies easier access to capital markets. The new rules include instructions for the completion of registration, annual, quarterly, and other periodic reporting forms for companies qualifying as small business issuers. Two registration forms are available to a qualified small business issuer, Form SB-1 and Form SB-2, either of which may be used to register securities to be sold for cash. The SB-1 has a $10 million limitation.

The small business issuer rules and forms replaced the requirements under Form S-18, the previous alternative for registering an offering intended for a smaller enterprise. Form S-18 contained a $7.5 million limit.

To qualify as a small business issuer, a company must satisfy the following conditions:

- The company must be a U.S. or Canadian company.
- Revenues must be less than $25 million a year.
- The aggregate market value of equity securities held by noncontrolling persons (the public float) must be less than $25 million.
- The company cannot be an investment company.
- If the issuing company is a majority-owned subsidiary, the parent company must also qualify as a small business issuer.

All small business issuers can use Form SB-2. Form SB-1 is available if a small business issuer has not registered more than $10 million in securities offerings in any continuous 12-month period, including the transaction being registered.

The SB-1 and SB-2 have fewer specified disclosures than the S-1 and require two years of audited financial statements, compared to the three years of audited financial statements needed for the S-1. The SB-1 permits the choice of using a question-and-answer format or a traditional narrative format. The alternative question-and-answer format is the same model available in Regulation A filings. The determination as to whether a company already reporting under the 1934 Act is a small business issuer is based on its revenues during its last fiscal year and its public float as of a date within 60 days of the date the registration statement is filed. In the case of an IPO, the public float is based on the number of shares outstanding prior to the offering and the estimated public offering price. Once the small business issuer becomes a reporting company, it can remain as such until it exceeds the revenue limit or the public float limit for two consecutive years.

As a result of the higher limit and the eased compliance burden, the SB-2 has been a popular form for IPOs where the company qualifies as a small business issuer. The SB-1 has been used infrequently, probably because any compliance savings compared to the SB-2 are not considered significant in relation to the offering limits of $10 million. Many underwriters require more information than is required in the SB-1.

See Appendix A at the end of this chapter, which compares certain key requirements of the S-1, the SB-2, the SB-1, and the Regulation A offering circular.

MANAGEMENT'S DISCUSSION AND ANALYSIS (MD&A)

The SEC considers the MD&A to be a very important disclosure section of the registration statements and reporting forms filed. The objective, as stated in a 1987 release, is to provide a narrative explanation that would enable investors to judge the quality of earnings and the likelihood that past performance is indicative of future performance. MD&A is intended to give the investor an opportunity to look at the company through the eyes of management.

The MD&A requires discussion of any known trends, events, or uncertainties that have or are reasonably likely to have a material impact on liquidity, capital resources, net sales or revenues, or income from continuing operations. Among the matters described, the MD&A should include: (1) internal and external sources of liquidity, (2) material commitments for capital expenditures and the expected sources of funds for such expenditures, and (3) the causes of material changes from period to period in the financial statements. Descriptions and amounts of matters that would have an impact on future operations and have not had an impact in the past, and of matters that have had an impact on reported operations and are not expected to have an impact on future earnings, are important as indicators of to what extent reported financial information may not be indicative of future operating results or financial condition.

Appendix A

COMPARISON OF CERTAIN DISCLOSURE REQUIREMENTS— FORMS SB-2, SB-1, S-1, AND REGULATION A

	Registration on Form			Offering Statement under Regulation A Exemption
	SB-2	SB-1	S-1	
Issuer qualifications	Qualifying SBI	Qualifying SBI	N/A	(1)
Size of offering	(2)	$10 million in any continuous 12-month period	No limit	$5 million per year (limited to $1.5 million by selling shareholders)
Financial statements(3)	One balance sheet, two years' statements of income and cash flows (audited)	One balance sheet, two years' statements of income and cash flows (audited)	Two balance sheets, three years' statements of income and cash flows (audited)	One balance sheet, two statements of income and cash flows (unaudited, unless audited statements are available)
Requirements	Regulation S-B (tracks Regulation S-K with major differences noted below)	Regulation S-B and Form 1-A (question-and-answer format available as alternative)	Regulation S-K	Form 1-A (question-and-answer format available as alternative)
Selected financial data	N/A	N/A	Selected financial data must be presented for five years	N/A

Appendix A *(continued)*

	Registration on Form			Offering Statement under Regulation A Exemption
	SB-2	SB-1	S-1	
Management's discussion and analysis	Two years	Of certain relevant factors up to two years	Three years	Of certain relevant factors up to two years
Description of business	Developments during last three years	Developments during last five years	Developments during last five years	Developments during last five years
Supplemental schedules	Not required	Not required	Certain specified schedules are required	Not required
Quarterly data	Not required	Not required	Required for certain companies	Not required
Certain relationships and related transactions	Two years	Two years	Five years	Two years
Other				Testing the waters provisions(4)

Notes:

(1) A nonreporting U.S. or Canadian company that is not an investment company nor a development company with no specific business plan qualifies for the Regulation A exemption. Can be used by companies not qualifying as a small business issuer. Can be disqualified under "bad boy provisions" (prior offenses).

(2) No limitation on the size of the offering under the SB-2 is stated. However, to qualify as a small business issuer, the public float is limited to $25 million. Therefore, the size of the offering is effectively limited to $25 million, less existing public float.

(3) If financial statements are as of a date 135 days or more prior to the effective date, interim financial statements (unaudited) are required. Regulation A filings require interim financials if filing takes place more than 90 days (six months with permission) after year-end.

(4) Can solicit, under prescribed conditions, indications of interest in a contemplated Regulation A offering before filing offering circular.

Appendix B
KEY STEPS IN THE IPO PROCESS

Key Steps in the IPO Process

Stages		1	2	3	4	5	6	7	8	9	10	11	12	13	14
												Week			
Phase 1	Due diligence	x	x	x											
	Draft registration statement	x	x	x	x										
Phase 2	Initial filing with SEC				x										
	Prepare road show and marketing materials					x	x								
Phase 3	Receive comments from SEC							x	x	x	x				
	Print and distribute red herrings									x	x				
	Road show presentations										x	x			
Phase 4	Pricing of IPO													x	
	File final prospectus with SEC													x	
	Closing of IPO														x

Chapter Six

After You're Public

Rosenman & Colin

ENTREPRENEUR'S OVERVIEW

After a company registers and sells securities under the Securities Act of 1933 (the Securities Act), it is required, under the Exchange Act of 1934 (the Exchange Act), to file periodic reports and reports of events or transactions of major significance with the SEC. Should a company either list a class of securities on a national exchange (a listed company), or should a class of its equity securities be held by 500 or more shareholders and its total assets reach $5 million or more (a Section 12(g) company), it becomes subject to registration and certain other requirements under the Exchange Act, regardless of whether it has been required to file a registration statement under the Securities Act.

The Securities Act registration regulates the sale or distribution to the public of specified quantities of securities. A company may be required to file a Securities Act registration more than once, depending on how many times it has a public sale or distribution of securities. The Exchange Act registration covers a whole class of equity securities and occurs once (unless terminated [see later discussion] and reinstated).

The other or additional provisions for listed and section 12(g) companies include:

- Regulations governing proxy solicitations and annual reports to stockholders.
- Regulations that require directors, officers, and shareholders who beneficially own more than 10 percent of certain classes of equity securities (insiders) to file reports with the SEC on their ownership and changes in ownership of the stock and to turn over any profits to the

company made within six months on trading in any of the company's equity securities (short swing profits). The insiders are also prohibited from selling any of the company's equity securities unless they actually own such securities and deliver them within a short specified time after sale (short sale prohibition).

- Requirements that beneficial owners of over 5 percent of the class of equity securities listed, or of the class that caused the company to register under Section 12(g), file certain reports with the company, the SEC, and the exchange on which it is listed, if any. The basic purpose is to provide information concerning potential tender offers.

The following are also covered in this chapter:

- Prohibitions against trading in securities if the trader is in possession of material nonpublic information. These prohibitions apply even if the trader is not a director, officer, significant stockholder, or employee.
- Criteria under Rule 144 of the Securities Act for the sale of restricted securities and securities owned by significant security holders, directors, and officers (affiliates).
- Listing requirements and compliance requirements after listing.
- The role of a market maker.
- Going private or reducing ownership so that the company is not subject to periodic reporting, proxy, or other applicable rules.
- Electronic transmission (EDGAR).

Not every regulation applicable to public companies, or exemption therefrom, is described in this chapter. Each company that has gone public or otherwise becomes subject to the requirements of the Exchange Act should obtain advice from competent securities counsel as to particular regulations applicable to it.

PERIODIC REPORTING REQUIREMENTS

Companies subject to the SEC reporting requirements (reporting companies) are required to report on their financial results and operations annually on Form 10-K and quarterly on Form 10-Q and to report any event or transaction of major significance on Form 8-K. Form 10-K is to be filed within 90 days after the end of each fiscal year of the company. Form 10-Q is filed within 45 days after the end of the first three fiscal quarters of each fiscal year. It is not filed for the fourth quarter of the fiscal year. Form 8-K must be filed within specified periods following the occurrence of certain events.

A qualified small business issuer (SBI) (see Chapter Five) may file Forms 10-KSB and 10-QSB in lieu of Forms 10-K and 10-Q, respectively. These forms require slightly less disclosure.

Forms 10-K and 10-KSB

Form 10-K is a detailed report requiring audited financial statements as well as extensive descriptions of the company's activities, operations, and other events affecting its business during the preceding fiscal year. Form 10-K is presented in four parts.

Part I requires narrative descriptions regarding the business and activities of the company. It also requires information regarding property holdings of the company, material lawsuits to which the company is a party or which could affect any of its property, and matters on which the company's stockholders have voted during the fourth quarter.

Part II requires information of a more quantitative nature. The company must provide information about the market for its securities. It must also furnish selected financial data and management's discussion and analysis of the financial condition and results of operations (MD&A). As described in Chapter Five, the SEC has consistently emphasized the importance of the MD&A. In an interpretive release, the SEC stated that the purpose was to give investors a look at the company through the eyes of management by providing a historical and prospective analysis of the financial conditions and results of operations.

The 10-KSB does not require selected financial data.

In part III, the company furnishes information concerning its directors, officers, and major security holders. It must disclose executive compensation and describe transactions entered into by the company with its directors, officers, or major security holders.

The executive compensation disclosure requirements were recently revised to use a series of tables and charts to present the elements (e.g., salary, bonuses, options, etc.) and extent of compensation of the chief executive officer and up to four of the most highly compensated officers. In addition, the directors (or an appropriate subcommittee) must include a board compensation committee report that, among other matters, explains the policies governing the compensation to executive officers and the specific relationship of corporate performance to the compensation, with particular emphasis on the criteria relating to the chief executive's compensation. Small business issuers are exempt from many of these disclosure requirements, including exemption from the board compensation committee report.

Part IV consists of exhibits, financial statements and schedules, and a description of any Form 8-K filings made during the last quarter. Many of the required exhibits need not be filed if they have been previously filed with the SEC and reference is made to such prior filings.

The financial statements and notes thereto must be audited and accompanied by a report of the independent public accountants who performed the audit. The financial statements include balance sheets at the end of the two previous years and statements of income and cash flows for each of the three previous years and specified supplemental schedules.

The 10-KSB requires one balance sheet and statements of income and cash flows for each of the two previous years and does not require any supplemental schedules.

Forms 10-Q and 10-QSB

Form 10-Q requires less disclosure than Form 10-K. Part I of Form 10-Q calls for unaudited financial statements and the company's MD&A, including explanations of material changes in revenue and expense items in the relevant quarter and the current year to date, as compared to the same quarter in the prior fiscal year and the same period in the prior fiscal year. The quarterly financial statements are condensed. Much of the prior year-end disclosures are not duplicated. Part II includes disclosure of new developments in the quarter of any: (1) material litigation in which the company is a party or which might affect any of its property, (2) changes in the rights of any class of registered securities, (3) defaults on debt or securities that are registered or senior to registered securities, (4) matters on which security holders have voted, and (5) Form 8-K filings that occurred or were made during the quarter with respect to which the Form 10-Q is being filed.

The Form 10-QSB requires essentially the same information as Form 10-Q, except that the requirements for MD&A can differ.

Form 8-K

Form 8-K is filed upon the occurrence of certain events the SEC considers important to security holders. Events required to be disclosed on Form 8-K are changes in control of the company, the resignation of public accountants, the resignation of directors due to disagreements with the company that the resigning directors request be disclosed, the acquisition or disposition of a significant amount of assets, matters relating to bankruptcy or receivership proceedings, and changes in the company's fiscal year. Other events, not specifically called for on the form, may be disclosed if the company should consider such events to be important to security holders.

The timing for filing depends on the event, but generally the form is required to be filed rapidly after the event giving rise to the filing occurs. Filing times vary between five business days or 15 calendar days after the occurrence of the event giving rise to the filing. Current and pro forma financial information must be provided for major acquisitions or dispositions (see Chapter Eight). Extensions in time may be obtained, if necessary, to provide audited statements of acquired businesses.

Termination of Reporting Requirements

Unless a company has a class of securities listed on a national securities exchange, it may elect to terminate its obligations to file the periodic reports if either: (a) each class of its equity securities is held of record by fewer than 300 persons, or (b) each class of its equity securities is held of record by fewer than 500 persons and it has had total assets of not more than $5 million on the last day of each of its three most recent fiscal years. Some companies may choose to reacquire some of their securities in order to terminate the reporting obligations if they have only slightly over the number of security holders referenced above. The SEC regulates such reacquisition, as discussed later in this chapter.

PROXY SOLICITATIONS AND ANNUAL REPORTS TO SECURITY HOLDERS

Listed companies and section 12(g) companies must comply with certain rules regulating the solicitation of proxies or written consents from their security holders. Companies required to file periodic reports solely because they have conducted registered offerings under the Securities Act are not subject to the proxy and annual report to security holder rules.

In most instances, companies subject to the proxy solicitation rules may solicit proxies or written consents only when they furnish each security holder being solicited, at the time of the initial solicitation, a preliminary or definitive proxy statement containing information required by the SEC's detailed proxy rules.

The preliminary proxy statement and form of proxy must be filed with the SEC at least 10 days before distribution to security holders, unless the materials relate solely to the uncontested election of directors or other specified routine matters. The SEC may or may not review the filing. Definitive proxy materials must be filed with the SEC at the time they are first sent to security holders. The SEC must also receive copies of all materials being distributed as part of the solicitation.

The SEC has set forth rules governing the inclusion of proposals made by a security holder. A security holder wishing to conduct his or her own proxy or written consent solicitation may require the company to furnish a list of the names and addresses of security holders eligible to vote or to mail proxy materials, at his or her expense, to such security holders. Special rules exist for both the company and security holders engaged in an election contest.

Even if a company elects not to solicit proxies with respect to any meeting of its security holders, if such company is subject to the proxy rules, it must furnish security holders with an information statement containing substantially the same information that would be required in a proxy statement if proxies were to be solicited. Preliminary and definitive copies of the information statement must be filed with SEC.

Regardless of whether proxies are solicited, if directors are to be elected at a security holders' meeting or by their written consents, the company must furnish the security holders with an annual report, including audited financial statements. The report shall contain the company's MD&A and information about its business, industry, directors and executive officers, and securities, in each case in such detail as prescribed by the SEC. Copies of the annual report must be sent to the SEC.

TRADING ON NONPUBLIC INFORMATION

Section 10(b) of the Exchange Act has been interpreted to prohibit trading in securities if the trader is in possession of material nonpublic information. The trader does not need to be a director, officer, or substantial security holder in a company for the prohibition to apply; any person possessing significant information concerning a company that is not publicly known may not purchase or sell any of such company's securities.

Any seller violating this prohibition is liable to any contemporaneous purchaser of the same class of securities. It does not matter if the violator directly sells to or purchases from such contemporaneous trader. The amount of damages is the amount of profit gained or loss avoided by the violator, as measured by the price of the security a reasonable time after the inside information becomes publicly known. The contemporaneous trader may bring an action to recover such damages at any time within five years after the trade.

Any person who communicates material nonpublic information to a trader who subsequently violates the prohibition set forth above may also be liable for the damages described above, even though such person did not engage in or benefit from any prohibited transaction.

In addition to contemporaneous traders, the SEC also may bring an action against any person who trades while in possession of material nonpublic information, furnishes such information to another who engages in such prohibited trading, or has control over another who engages in such prohibited trading. The SEC may seek an injunction against the prohibited conduct, seek to have the violator barred from ever serving as a director or officer of the company whose securities are the subject of the trade, or seek a penalty of up to three times the amount of profit gained or loss avoided (or $1 million, if greater, if the action is against a person having control over the violator). The SEC has five years from the time of the trade to bring such action.

These rules place a strong burden on companies and their management to ensure that their employees do not trade if they know nonpublic company information. Outside agents such as attorneys, accountants, and others may also incur liability if they or their employees trade based on nonpublic information about their clients.

EQUITY SECURITY TRANSACTIONS BY CERTAIN "INSIDERS"

In addition to the general prohibition against trading based on nonpublic information, listed companies and Section 12(g) companies are subject to Section 16 of the Exchange Act, which regulates trading in any of the company's equity securities by certain insiders. The purpose of the regulation is to prevent such persons from benefiting through security trades made at a time when they might be aware of material information affecting the company not known to the trading public.

The insiders consist of each of the company's directors and officers and each of the company's security holders beneficially owning more than 10 percent of any class of equity securities listed on a national exchange or causing the company to be a Section 12(g) company. The advice of securities counsel should be obtained to interpret what constitutes beneficial ownership and who is an officer. Once a person becomes subject to Section 16, the section regulates the person's interests in all of the company's equity securities owned by such person, regardless of whether they are listed or of the class that caused the company to be a Section 12(g) company.

The Section 16 regulations essentially impose three requirements. The first requires directors, officers, and 10 percent owners to report to the SEC on their holdings of and trading in any of the company's equity securities. The second requires directors, officers, and 10 percent owners to turn over to the company any profits they realize from a purchase followed by a sale, or a sale followed by a purchase, of any of the company's equity securities made within any six-month period. The third enjoins directors, officers, and 10 percent owners from selling any of the company's equity securities unless they actually own such securities and deliver them within a short specified time after sale.

Reporting Requirements

Directors, officers, and 10 percent owners subject to Section 16 must file:

- Form 3, indicating their beneficial ownership of any of the company's equity securities at such time as the company becomes a listed company or Section 12(g) company or within 10 days after they acquire the position triggering their Section 16 reporting requirements if this occurs after the company becomes a listed company or Section 12(g) company.

- Form 4 within 10 days after the end of any calendar month during which there was any change in their equity security beneficial ownership to report such change. Extensions are available for small acquisitions.

- Form 5 within 45 days after the end of the company's fiscal year (if it is subject to the reporting requirements at any time during such year) to report any transaction not previously reported on Form 4, either because of a relevant exemption or due to failure to report.

Derivative securities, or securities convertible or exercisable for other securities, are considered to be of the same class as the underlying securities into or for which they can be converted or exercised. Acquisitions or dispositions of derivative securities are to be reported separately from acquisitions or dispositions of the underlying securities. The conversion or exercise is to be reported as a purchase or sale of the underlying security, as the case may be, and a closing of the derivative security position.

Turnover of Short-Swing Profits

If a director, officer, or 10 percent owner, subject to Section 16, makes a profit from a purchase of any equity securities of his or her company followed by a sale of equity securities of the same class, or a sale of equity securities of his or her company followed by a purchase of the same class of equity securities, within a six month period (a short-swing profit), he or she must turn over the profit to the company. A short-swing profit is deemed to occur if the sale is made for a price greater than the purchase price and is determined based on the lesser of the quantity of securities sold or purchased. Once this quantity is determined, the lowest purchase prices paid for such quantity of securities are aggregated and then subtracted from the aggregate of the highest sales prices received for the sale of such quantity to determine the short-swing profit.

There are specific rules concerning the increase or decrease in the ownership of derivative securities, such as options and warrants. Certain specified transactions are exempt from the short-swing profit rules.

The company may sue to recover the short-swing profits to which it is entitled under Section 16. If it fails to do so, any of its security holders may sue in its name and on its behalf. Suit must be brought within two years of the event giving rise to the short-swing profit.

Short-Sale Prohibition

Any director, officer, or 10 percent owner subject to Section 16 is enjoined from selling any equity security unless he or she owns such security, he or she deposits such security in the mail (or delivers it to other transportation headed toward the purchaser) within five days of the sale, and it is actually received by the purchaser within 20 days of the sale.

REPORTING REQUIREMENTS FOR SIGNIFICANT ACQUISITIONS OF EQUITY SECURITIES

If a company is a listed company or Section 12(g) company, any beneficial owner of over 5 percent of the class of equity securities causing the company to have such status must file a report with the SEC and the company for the purpose of providing information about potential tender offers.

If such percentage ownership arises pursuant to an acquisition made after the company has become a listed company or Section 12(g) company, then, subject to limited exceptions, the report must be filed within 10 days of such acquisition. The report must comply with the SEC's Schedule 13D requirements and contain certain information concerning the beneficial owner; the source and amount of funds for the acquisition; the purpose of the acquisition, including any plans or proposals the beneficial owner may have for future purchases of securities of the company or plans for any major change for the company (such as liquidation, sale of assets, merger or consolidation, or changes in the board of directors or in the company's dividend policy or capitalization); the amount and nature of the owner's beneficial ownership; and whether the owner has any agreement, arrangement, or understanding affecting any of the company's securities.

If the 5 percent beneficial ownership existed prior to the time the company becomes a listed company or Section 12(g) company, if the acquisition was obtained through a registered securities offering, or if the owner's total acquisitions within the preceding 12 months amount to not more than 2 percent of the class, the beneficial owner only needs to file a report within 45 days after the end of the calendar year during which the company became a listed or Section 12(g) company, or the acquisition occurred, as the case may be. This report must follow the SEC's Schedule 13G. It includes the name of the beneficial owner and the amount and nature of his beneficial ownership.

SALE OF RESTRICTED SECURITIES AND SECURITIES OWNED BY AFFILIATES

As noted in Chapter Four, securities may be subject to resale restrictions if acquired pursuant to an exempt offering. In addition, regardless of whether securities are subject to resale restrictions, if they are owned by an affiliate of the company that issued them, such affiliate may be deemed an underwriter, in which event an offer of the securities by such affiliate may require registration under the Securities Act.

An affiliate of a company is defined as any person or entity who directly or indirectly, through one or more intermediaries, controls, is controlled by, or is under common control with the company. Significant security holders, directors, and officers may be considered affiliates.

Rule 144

The SEC has promulgated Rule 144 under the Securities Act, which sets forth certain criteria for such security sales. If the criteria are satisfied, securities otherwise subject to resale restrictions may be sold without registration, and affiliates may sell securities they own in their company without being deemed underwriters. The Rule 144 criteria are based on the availability of public information concerning the company whose securities are to be sold, holding periods before sales may occur, limits on the amount of securities that may be sold, restrictions on the manner in which the securities may be sold, and filing requirements.

Public Information Requirement

Rule 144 may only be relied on if adequate public information is available concerning the company whose securities are to be sold. Usually, the company must have been subject to the

Exchange Act periodic reporting requirements for at least 90 days and must have filed all required reports for the shorter of the time it has been subject to the reporting requirements, or the preceding 12 months. If the company is not subject to the periodic reporting requirements, information concerning the company must be publicly available, including the name of the company's chief executive officer and board members, the company's most recent balance sheet and profit and loss and retained earnings statements, similar financial statements for its last two fiscal years, and, in certain cases, information about the seller of the securities.

Holding Period

The seller must have owned and paid for the securities for at least two years prior to the Rule 144 sale. Special rules exist if the seller purchases the securities by note or through an installment sale. Tacking rules exist in certain instances that extend the period during which securities are deemed to be owned. Securities acquired by a security holder from stock dividends, splits, or conversions are deemed owned by the security holder during the period the security holder owned the underlying security. Securities acquired by a security holder by pledge, gift, or inheritance are deemed owned by the security holder during the period they were owned by the pledgor, donor, or decedent.

Limits on Amount Sold

Sales of any class of a company's securities made by an affiliate of the company during any three-month period may not exceed the greater of (1) 1 percent of the outstanding securities in such class, (2) the average weekly reported volume of trading in such class on a national securities exchange or automated interdealer quotation system of a registered national securities association (such as NASDAQ) during the preceding four weeks, or (3) the average weekly trading volume reported for such class through a consolidated reporting transaction system. The same restrictions apply with respect to resales of restricted securities by non-affiliates unless the seller was not an affiliate at any time during the three-month sale period or the three months prior thereto and has owned the securities being sold for three years.

Special rules require holders of securities acquired through conversion, pledge, gift, or inheritance to include sales of convertible securities or sales made by pledgors, donors, or decedents, as appropriate, in applying the quantity limits set forth above. The same restrictions apply to nonaffiliate sales unless the seller was not an affiliate at any time during the three months before the sale and owned the securities being sold for at least three years.

Manner of Sale

Securities sold by affiliates pursuant to Rule 144 must be sold in brokers' transactions or in transactions with market makers. Neither the seller, broker, nor market maker is allowed to solicit sales. The seller may only pay a regular broker's commission. The same restrictions apply to nonaffiliate sales unless the seller was not an affiliate at any time during the three months before the sale and owned the securities being sold for at least three years.

Filing Requirements

If, during any three-month period, an affiliate sells more than 500 shares or units in any class of securities, or securities in any class for an aggregate sales price exceeding $10,000, the affiliate must file with the SEC a notice of the sales on Form 144. The same notice requirement is applicable to nonaffiliate sales unless the seller was not an affiliate at any time during such three-month sale period or for three months prior thereto and owned all the securities sold for at least three years.

LISTING

Listing Requirements

Listing a company on a national securities exchange or on the National Association of Securities Dealers Automated Quotation (NASDAQ) system enhances the marketability of a security mainly because it is easier for investors to follow the stock. Companies that do not desire to or cannot qualify for a listing are relegated to the "pink-sheets," a privately printed list of price quotes from brokers who subscribe to the pink sheets. The NASDAQ and the New York (NYSE) and American Stock Exchange (AMEX) listings are published daily in *The Wall Street Journal* and in many general newspapers. Selected stock quotes from the pink sheets are published less frequently. Most companies that have completed an IPO and that qualify for a listing opt for a NASDAQ listing, frequently on the small cap market listing. As an enterprise matures, it may qualify for the NASDAQ national market or an exchange listing.

A company's securities generally will not be listed unless the company can demonstrate a sufficient level of trading in such securities, fairly widespread security ownership, significant assets, and profitability. The illustration at the end of this chapter compares certain of the numerical listing requirements of NASDAQ, the AMEX, and the NYSE.

Other factors are considered in determining whether a security qualifies. The New York Stock Exchange will consider factors such as national interest in the company, the character of the market for the company's products, its relative stability and position in the industry, and whether it is engaged in an expanding industry and appears able to maintain its position in such industry. The NYSE will also review stockholder voting rights, voting arrangements, control situations, and related party transactions. The AMEX will generally consider the nature of the issuing company's business, the market for its products, the reputation of its management, its historical record and pattern of growth, its financial integrity, its demonstrated earnings power, and its future outlook. NASDAQ reserves the right to request and review other information concerning the company seeking a NASDAQ listing.

Compliance Requirements

Once its securities are accepted for listing, the company must comply with the regulations of the exchange or NASDAQ, which are fairly detailed and often dovetail with the SEC regulations.

Failure to comply can result in suspension of trading in or delisting of a company's securities. The compliance requirements include matters such as furnishing financial statements to stockholders, maintenance of audit committees, maintenance of transfer agents and registrars, and the holding of annual stockholder meetings.

In addition, if a company falls below specified numeric levels of items, such as number of shares publicly held, net income, market value of publicly held shares, net tangible assets, and stockholders' equity, consideration will be given to suspending or delisting a security. The numeric items are generally the same as those considered for original listing but at lower levels.

MARKET MAKERS

Certain dealers act as "market makers" to create and maintain a market for those securities in which they elect to deal. The Exchange Act defines a market maker as a specialist in a particular security acting as a dealer in such security, a dealer acting as a block positioner for a particular security, or a dealer who indicates he or she is willing to buy and sell a particular security on a regular or continuous basis. Generally, any dealer who conducts his or her purchases and sales in a particular security in a manner that generates a primary or secondary market for such security comes within this definition of market maker.

A market maker may own over 10 percent of the class of securities in which he or she deals and is exempt from the short-swing profit turnover and sale delivery requirements of Section 16 of the Exchange Act, as long as the securities are held in the ordinary course of business (and not in an investment account) for the purpose of stabilizing a market, other than on an exchange, for the securities.

Certain market makers who satisfy the requirements for being a qualified OTC market maker, qualified third market maker, or qualified block positioner, as set forth in the Exchange Act, may obtain loans to purchase securities to be secured by the securities purchased without regard to the margin requirements established under the Federal Reserve Board's Regulation U, which limits ordinary margin loans to 50 percent of the value of the securities being purchased.

Because of their ability to obtain credit without regard to the margin requirements and to buy and sell blocks of securities without regard to the short-swing profit rules, market makers exert a major influence over the securities in which they deal. Companies seeking active trading will want to establish contact with a market maker. Having market makers will facilitate exchange or NASDAQ listing.

GOING PRIVATE

The SEC has promulgated rules to govern any solicitation by a company for the purchase of its own securities or for votes or consents of its security holders if the result, if successful, would be either to cause any class of its securities, the ownership of which requires the company to file periodic reports with the SEC, to be held of record by fewer than 300 persons or to cause any class of its securities to be delisted from a national securities exchange or NASDAQ.

Neither the company nor any of its affiliates may engage in any such solicitation unless the company or affiliate files with the SEC a report on Schedule 13E-3 and all necessary amendments thereto, including an amendment within 10 days following the end of such solicitation to report the results, and discloses the information in such report to all security holders of the class being solicited at least 20 days prior to the proposed purchase or vote.

The report must contain information about the security to be affected, including its price during the prior two years, the purchaser, terms of the proposed transaction, future plans for the company (similar to what needs to be described pursuant to Schedule 13D, discussed previously), source of funds, reasons for and alternatives to the proposed transaction, information as to the fairness of the transaction, including the views of any dissenting directors and the findings in any outside reports or appraisals, the positions to be taken by directors, officers, or affiliates in the transaction, and audited, annual, interim, and, if appropriate, pro forma financial information.

Should the company wish to make a tender offer for its own securities, the SEC rules are even more detailed.

National securities exchanges and NASDAQ also have their own regulations dealing with transactions that result in delisting of securities.

ELECTRONIC TRANSMISSIONS

Most of the documents described in this chapter that must be filed with the SEC are now required to be filed electronically, rather than by submission on paper. Filings may be made by use of magnetic tape, diskette, or direct transmission.

The SEC requires all registration statements required under either the Securities Act or the Exchange Act, periodic reports, proxy materials, and schedules relating to substantial acquisitions (Schedule 13D or 13G) or going-private transactions (Schedule 13E-3) to be filed electronically.

Not all filings are currently to be made electronically. Forms 3, 4, and 5 are still to be filed in paper form, as are certain documents requesting confidentiality. Filings made in the SEC's regional offices are also to be done on paper. Annual reports to security holders filed for the SEC's information may be made either electronically or on paper. The electronic filing system is called Electronic Data Gathering Analysis and Retrieval, or EDGAR. The SEC produces an EDGAR manual to aid in filing. The SEC has adopted certain rules relating to the format for electronic filings. These relate to the use of tabular or columnar formats, capitalization when bold type is required, and typed signatures, among other items. Manual signatures authenticating the typed ones must be maintained in the company's files for five years after each filing.

Current penalties for failure to file electronically are not very severe. They merely limit the ability to use certain procedures in future filings and extend tender offer times. Hardship exemptions from electronic filings are available to a limited extent. Clearly, however, electronic filing is expected, and the penalties for failure to use it are likely to become more onerous.

Appendix
COMPARISON OF LISTING REQUIREMENTS—SELECTED NUMERICAL CRITERIA

	NASDAQ National Market		NASDAQ Small Cap Market	AMEX Regular (common stock)
	Alternative I	*Alternative II*		
Net tangible assets	$4,000,000	$12,000,000		
Total stockholders' equity			$2,000,000	$4,000,000
Total assets			$4,000,000	
Net income	$ 400,000(a)			
Pre-tax income	$ 750,000(a)			$ 750,000(a)(d)
Publicly held shares	500,000	1,000,000	100,000	500,000 or 1,000,000(c)
Aggregate market value of publicly held shares	$3,000,000	$15,000,000	$1,000,000	$3,000,000(d)
Average monthly trading volume— preceding six months				
Minimum per share bid price	$5	$3	$3	$3
Number of public stockholders	(800)(b) (or 400)(b)	400	300	800 or 400(c)

AMEX
Emerging Company Marketplace

Traded on NASDAQ		Not Traded on NASDAQ	
Alternative I	*Alternative II*	*Alternative I*	*Alternative II*
$1,000,000	$2,000,000	$2,000,000	$2,000,000
$2,000,000	$2,000,000	$4,000,000	$3,000,000
250,000	250,000	250,000	40,000
$2,500,000	$2,500,000	$2,500,000	Above $10,000,000
$1	Below $1	$3	$2
300	300	300	300

		NYSE
Net tangible assets		$18,000,000(f)
Total stockholders' equity		
Total assets		
Net income		
Pre-tax income	Latest year	$ 2,500,000
	Each of 2 preceding years	$ 2,000,000 (e)
Publicly held shares		1,100,000
Aggregate market value of publicly held shares		$18,000,000(f)
Average monthly trading volume— preceding six months		100,000 shares
Minimum per share bid price		
Number of public stockholders		2,000

Notes:

(a) Either in the latest fiscal year or in two of the last three years.

(b) 800 shareholders if one million or fewer shares are publicly held; but only 400 shareholders if the average daily trading is at least 2,000 shares or more than one million shares are publicly held.

(c) If held by at least 800 shareholders, the minimum distribution is 500,000 shares. If held by at least 400 shareholders, the minimum distribution is one million shares.

(d) A company that does not satisfy the minimum income requirements may still have a class of securities listed if the company can demonstrate that it has sufficient financial resources to continue operations over an extended period of time, it is regarded as suitable by the AMEX, and it meets the following numerical criteria. The company must have three years of operations and a stockholders' equity of at least $4 million, it must satisfy the public distribution requirements, and its publicly held shares must have a minimum per share price of $3 and an aggregate market value of $15 million. A company will be considered on this basis depending on the nature and scope of its operations, its financial condition, its assets, its management, and its industry.

(e) Or, alternatively, $4.5 million for the latest fiscal year and at least $6.5 million total for the last three fiscal years, each of which must have been profitable.

(f) Either market value of publicly held shares or net tangible assets must equal $18 million.

Chapter Seven

Other Financing Sources

ENTREPRENEUR'S OVERVIEW

The following other financing sources and the circumstances that lead to their use are reviewed in this chapter:

- An employee stock ownership plan can result in a more highly motivated workforce and enable its owners to realize and diversify some of their investment with the potential to defer capital gains tax.
- Equity swaps, a relatively new type of transaction, may be used in limited circumstances to assist a major shareholder in a public company to diversify his or her investment without giving up control or paying capital gains tax.
- The world has gotten smaller because of technology advances. As a result, a worldwide financial market has been created. An enterprise should consider financing from foreign sources if it is cheaper or not readily available in the United States.
- Franchising as a means of marketing a product or a business format can furnish the capital to meet the costs of opening new units and be the means to rapid expansion.
- Merging with a public shell can provide a more rapid and less costly road to becoming a public company. But caution is important, as many shells have turned out not to be public companies, to be in violation of securities law, and to have undisclosed liabilities.

- Venture capital firms can be useful as a source of
  financing for companies that cannot obtain additional debt
  financing from banks or other financial institutions and
  are not ready for a public offering.

EMPLOYEE STOCK OWNERSHIP PLAN (ESOP)

An ESOP is a type of retirement plan designed to invest primarily in the sponsors'stock. Since an ESOP is a retirement plan, the Employee Retirement Income Security Act (ERISA) applies. Accordingly, plan assets are separate from the employer corporation and placed in a trust. ESOPs can serve several purposes, such as to provide a vehicle for the employees to obtain an interest in the employer corporation, provide retirement funds to employees, or to finance the owners' sale of stock. Subchapter S corporations, partnerships, and proprietors are not eligible to establish ESOPs.

In the simplest format, the employer corporation makes tax-deductible contributions to the trust, which are used to purchase shares of the corporation, either from the shareholders, the company, or in the open market. The company can also contribute stock directly to the ESOP.

Alternatively, the ESOP borrows from the sponsoring employer (internally leveraged ESOP) or from a financial institution (externally leveraged ESOP). It uses the borrowed funds to purchase the company's stock, either from existing shareholders, in the open market, or from the company. The company is invariably required to guarantee any outside loan, as the ESOP is dependent on the employer corporation for funds to repay the loan. Tax-deductible contributions by the corporation to the ESOP and, if certain criteria are met, tax-deductible dividends on the employer's stock are used to pay both principal and interest. The repayments of principal as well as interest thereby become tax-deductible.

As interest and principal payments are made on the ESOP debt, the stock acquired by the ESOP is allocated to the accounts of individual employees. Employees vest in their allocated shares over a period no longer than seven years. Employees receive their vested shares when they leave. A closely held company must offer to purchase the shares of departing employees at fair value. The company can exercise a right of first refusal if the employee elects to sell his or her shares elsewhere.

The price that an ESOP pays for the company stock must be based on the fair market value or on an annual appraisal by an independent appraiser. Paying more than the fair value can subject the trustee to liability for the overpayment and an excise tax to be imposed on the shareholders or the company.

Lenders can exclude 50 percent of the interest income they receive from the loans to the ESOP if the ESOP owns more than 50 percent of the sponsoring company's stock. The lending institution will usually share a part of this savings in the form of lower interest rates on the ESOP loan.

Dividends on the ESOP shares used by the ESOP to repay a loan are deductible by the employer if the proceeds of the loan were used to acquire the stock on which the dividends are paid. The dividend deductions are not subject to the contribution limitations based on payroll.

A selling shareholder can defer tax on the gain from the sale of his or her stock to the ESOP once the ESOP owns 30 percent of the employer's stock if:

- The selling shareholder reinvests in bonds or stocks of U.S. domestic corporations (replacement securities) within a period from three months before to 12 months after the sale of the stock to the ESOP. Securities of real estate trusts, mutual funds, or other passive investments do not qualify as replacement securities.
- The selling shareholder has held the stock of the employer corporation for at least three years prior to the sale.
- The selling shareholder consents to pay a 10 percent excise tax if the ESOP sells his or her former shares within a three-year period.

If the selling shareholder holds the replacement securities until death, the cost basis is stepped up to market value at the date of death, and no capital gains taxes are paid. The seller and his family are prohibited from participating in the acquired ESOP.

Other factors to be considered before establishing an ESOP are:

- The corporation's projected profits and cash flows should be sufficient to take advantage of the tax deduction for contributions and to provide cash for contributions or repayment of ESOP loans.

- Limitations on contributions are based on payroll. Contributions to other retirement plans will reduce the amount that can be contributed to the ESOP. There should be a large enough payroll to provide for coverage of loan payments.
- Ascertain that the existing debt structure or covenants in other loan agreements do not prevent the company from guaranteeing the ESOP debt.

Summary

In a closely held company, an ESOP affords the existing owners the opportunity to transfer ownership with a potential deferral of or avoidance of capital gains tax. From the employees' point of view, the business is bought without a personal investment and financed by a lower interest rate loan whose repayment is subsidized by a tax deduction. The employees may also retain greater job security than if the business was sold to outsiders.

As a financing vehicle for a company, where the ESOP winds up with a minority interest, the advantages are the tax savings resulting from the deduction of contributions necessary for payment of interest and loan principal and greater employee interest in the welfare of the company.

EQUITY SWAPS

A stockholder with a large holding in a public company may wish to diversify his or her investment. He or she may be unwilling or unable to sell his or her stock in the public company for one or more of the following reasons:

- A huge capital gains tax would result.
- The stockholder wishes to retain control or significant influence in the public company.

- Agreement on terms of a private sale cannot be reached.
- Under SEC rules, only a fraction of the holdings could be sold to the public without the company filing a registration statement.

The solution may be to enter into an equity swap. The stockholder enters into an agreement with a bank for a specified period of one to seven years whereby:

- The stockholder agrees to pay the bank any dividends from the stock during the specified period plus any appreciation in the value of the stock at the end of the period.
- The bank agrees to pay the stockholder a fixed rate of return on a fixed amount (the contractual amount) less a commission charged by the bank during the period, plus any loss in the value of the stock at the end of the period. The fixed amount is established at the fair value of the stock at the time the agreement is reached.

The stock is not exchanged or transferred. The stockholder retains ownership and the voting rights to his or her shares. The stockholder has swapped the risks and rewards of ownership, but not the ownership, in the shares for a fixed return over a defined period of time. The bank hedges its risk by selling the stock short or trading in options on the stock. Therefore, such a swap can only take place if the public float of the company is large enough to accommodate the short sales or option trading by the bank.

The shareholder is not limited to a swap for a fixed return on a contractual amount. He or she can, for example, swap for a basket of specific stocks, a floating rate return, or an index such as the S&P 500.

The general view is that an equity swap should not trigger a taxable gain or loss because beneficial ownership is retained. However, the Internal Revenue Service has not indicated what its position is on these swaps. There may also be uncertainty about the SEC's position on whether insider rules require disclosure. It is advisable to consult with your tax adviser and SEC counsel before entering into such a swap.

FOREIGN FINANCING

Advances in communications, travel, and computer technology have helped create a worldwide marketplace. Overseas capital markets, such as England and Japan, may offer debt or equity financing to middle-market companies at less cost or at times when it is not available in the United States.

How does a company locate foreign investors? One source is a U.S. investment banker that has overseas offices or relationships with foreign bankers. However, if the transaction is too small (less than 10 million), a large investment house will probably not be interested. The international affiliate or office of the company's accounting or law firm is another potential connection to foreign investment bankers. Further, many foreign bankers and investors have offices in the United States.

Private placements are more likely for the emerging company than public offerings. However, a profitable and growing company is an apt candidate for a public offering. If your company's product is sold in the foreign market, it will probably be a plus. London is the most likely location for an offering by a mid-sized U.S. company.

Offers and sales of securities that occur outside the United States do not require registration in the United States. Regulation S contains criteria used to determine whether offers and sales of securities qualify as being outside the United States. Regulation S establishes two sets of conditions (safe harbors). One set of conditions is applicable to offers and sales by issuers (the issuers' safe harbor), and the other is applicable to resales by persons other than the issuer (the resale safe harbor). If an offer and sale meet the conditions of the issuer safe harbor, or a resale meets the conditions of the resale safe harbor, the sale or resale is judged to be outside the United States and is not subject to registration under the Securities Act.

Two general conditions apply to all transactions. First, any offer or sale must be made in an "offshore transaction," as defined. Second, no "directed selling efforts," as defined, may be made in the United States in connection with an offer or sale. Other specific requirements must be met that depend on the existing circumstances.

FRANCHISING

Franchising is the sale of the usually exclusive right to operate a business or sell a product under the franchisor's name or trademark for a specified time period in a designated location or territory. Determining whether an arrangement is or is not a franchise under the various state laws sometimes requires careful analysis by legal counsel. Automobiles and gasoline are examples of products that are distributed through franchises. Business formats that have been successfully franchised include restaurants, hotels, lawn care, bookkeeping services, and weight-loss programs. Some franchises include previously established businesses, such as real estate brokers that converted to the franchisor's common system of marketing.

Advantages and Disadvantages

Some of the advantages of franchising are:

- Capital is provided to meet the costs of opening new outlets.
- Businesses are able to market their products on a regional and national basis.
- Growth is much more rapid than growth through addition of company-owned outlets.
- A franchisee who owns the business is usually more highly motivated than an employee-manager.
- The franchisee is liable for unpaid costs if the outlet fails.

Some of the disadvantages of franchising are:

- There is a potential for greater resistance to standard policies and controls by independent business owners than from company-employed managers.
- There is less flexibility in changing business strategies.
- Federal and state regulation of franchisors is time consuming and adds additional expense.
- Additional litigation tends to result from alleged breaches of franchise agreements or alleged misrepresentations at the time of the agreement.

Federal and State Regulation

A number of states have disclosure laws specifically designed to protect franchisees. Other states provide protection through general business laws. Federal regulation is provided by the Federal Trade Commission Rule (the Rule), which is titled "Disclosure Requirements and Prohibitions concerning Franchising and Business Opportunity Ventures." The Rule requires that any prospective franchisee be furnished with a written document containing minimum prescribed disclosures on or before the first personal meeting. State laws that require more extensive disclosure than the Rule take precedence. As a result, franchisors who register with states that have adopted the Uniform Franchise Offering Circular (UFOC) can furnish the UFOC to prospective franchisees in satisfaction of the Rule. Most of the states that have adopted the UFOC require registration with and approval by the state before a franchise can be offered within the state. There is no requirement to file with the Federal Trade Commission.

Areas of disclosure required by the Rule include the following:

- Business experience of the franchisor's key personnel.
- Business experience of the franchisor.
- History of litigation involving the franchisor, principals, and affiliates.
- Bankruptcy history of the franchisor, principals, and affiliates.
- Description of the franchise.
- Initial funds required to be paid by a franchisee.
- Recurring funds required to be paid by the franchisee.
- Persons from whom the franchisee is required to purchase, lease, or rent.
- Revenues to be received by the franchisor or its affiliates in consideration of goods or services purchased by a franchisee.
- Relationship between the franchisor and any supplier of goods and services to the franchise.
- Financing arrangements offered directly or indirectly by the franchisor.

- Forecasts of changes in the payments that the franchisee must make to the franchisor and to third parties to acquire and operate the business.
- Limitations on goods, services, customers, or areas.
- Other franchisors owned in common.
- Extent of personal participation required of the franchisee in the operation of the franchise.
- Terms and conditions of modification, termination, cancellation, and renewal of the franchise agreement.
- Data about franchises sold or discontinued by franchisees or terminated, not renewed, or acquired by the franchisor.
- Information concerning the number of franchises and company-owned outlets.
- Site selection.
- Nature, type, and cost of training provided.
- Public figure involvement.
- Financial information.
- Sales and earnings projections.

Because of the various bodies of law affecting franchising, it is advisable to engage an attorney experienced in this field.

Financial Statement Requirements

The FTC Rule requires a balance sheet for the franchisor's most recent fiscal year and an income statement and statement of cash flows for the last three fiscal years. If audited statements are not available, unaudited statements may be used. However, financial statements for the first year following the date when a disclosure statement is initially required must include an audited balance sheet. For each succeeding year thereafter, audited statements of income and cash flows would be added until three years of audited statements of income and cash flows, as well as an audited balance sheet at the latest fiscal year-end, are presented.

The UFOC, however, doesn't provide for such gradual introduction of audited financial statements. The UFOC requires an audited balance sheet as of the last fiscal year-end and audited statements of income and cash flows for each of the last three fiscal years at the outset. If the latest fiscal year-end financials are not within 90 days of the date of the filing, an unaudited balance sheet as of a date within 90 days of the filing date and unaudited statements of income and cash flow from the beginning of the year to the date of the unaudited balance sheet are also required.

Earnings Claims

Average or a range of actual or projected sales and earnings projections on an outlet basis (referred to as earnings claims) are not required. If none are made, a statement to that effect must be made. Franchisees, however, desire such information. Franchisors are reluctant to provide such data because of difficulty in complying with various federal and state definitions and standards and the potential for later claims of misrepresentation. If such data are presented, the franchisor must make market studies or statistical analyses available to the franchisee in order to substantiate the accuracy of the earnings claim. The data must be geographically relevant, and a "reasonable basis" to support the earnings claim must exist. The requirements for earnings claims under both the FTC Rule (for nonregulatory states) and under UFOC should be reviewed with legal counsel before deciding whether to provide such data.

Fees and Revenues

Among the fees earned by franchisors are the one-time initial fees for the sale of the right to develop and operate a single franchise unit or the sale of the right to develop a territory. Other fees include training fees, transfer fees if the franchisee sells the franchise, fees for managing construction projects for the franchisee, and fees when the franchisee exercises an option to renew. Recurring fees include royalties based on a percentage of gross receipts. A minimum annual royalty is often specified. Cooperative advertising charges to franchisees are usually also based on a percentage of sales. Depending on the nature of the franchise, revenues also result from the sale of product and the leasing of real estate and/or equipment to the franchises.

SHELL CORPORATIONS

Some closely held companies have gone public by merging with a public shell corporation. A public shell is an inactive corporation with a large number of shareholders. Some shells are companies whose activities have ceased. Other shell corporations result from blind pool offerings. In a blind pool offering, capital is raised through a public offering with no specific plans other than to acquire other businesses. The promoters of the shell locate a closely held company seeking to go public. The shell corporation issues stock for the stock of the closely held company. The stockholders of the closely held company usually wind up with a substantial majority of the public company. The percentage depends on the net assets of the shell and the value of the portion of the active closely held company that winds up in the hands of the stockholders of the shell. After the merger, the public company usually adopts the name of the closely held company so that identification of the operating company is maintained. For accounting purposes, the merger is treated similar to a reverse acquisition (see Chapter Eight).

The major advantage to the closely held company is that merger with a shell is less costly than the typical initial public offering. Some of the negative aspects of filing a registration statement are avoided. Most of the advantages of going public exist whether a company goes public "by the back door" or through a traditional IPO. One major exception is that if the shell has no or few net assets, no capital is raised. But the existence of a public market makes a private placement or a subsequent public offering easier.

However, there are caveats. Some shell companies have turned out to have undisclosed liabilities, not to be public companies, and/or to be in violation of various reporting or other provisions of federal securities law. Consultation with SEC counsel and investigation of the promoters is advisable.

VENTURE CAPITAL FIRMS

Venture capital firms provide equity financing for young companies with rapid growth potential or for mature companies that

are not eligible for additional debt financing and are not ready
for a public equity offering. They are usually partnerships of
wealthy individuals, pension funds, large corporations, and
foundations. Some large industrial companies and financial institutions have formed venture capital subsidiaries. Some venture capital firms specialize with regard to the type of
investment. Specialties include:

- Seed money for companies in the conceptual stage that are
  developing or have already developed a product.
- Start-up financing for companies that are ready to begin or
  have begun production and sales.
- Expansion financing for further product development,
  plant expansion, or expanded marketing costs.
- Bridge financing to cover a one- to two-year period until
  the company goes public.
- Acquisition financing.
- Companies in specific geographic areas and/or industries.

Each venture capital firm usually establishes minimum and
maximum investment amounts. The minimums can range from
$100,000 to $3 million and the maximum can range from $250,000
to $50 million. They are mainly interested in equity participa-
tions that will result in long-term capital gains within a five- to
seven-year period at an annual return of 40 percent or more. The
expectations are that the investment will be realized by selling
the company or through a public offering. See Chapter Two for
an example of how the expected realization is calculated.

The venture capital firm will participate in the management of
the company. The involvement is not on a day-to-day basis, but
includes activities such as assistance in obtaining debt financing,
recruiting management personnel, planning, and representation
on the board of directors.

Introductions to venture capital firms are best made by persons who are known to the venture capitalist. Bankers, lawyers,
accountants, and other businesspeople are likely sources for
names of firms. After the initial introduction and contact has
been made, a copy of the business plan (see Chapter Two) should
be forwarded to the venture capitalist. It may take three to six
months to get the financing.

As described in Chapter One, the *Corporate Finance Sourcebook*, published annually by National Register Publishing Company, catalogs sources of capital funding, including venture capital funds.

In addition to a seat or seats on the board of directors, the venture capital firm will want the right to obtain control of the board of directors and the right to replace the chief executive officer should the financial results fall below stipulated levels of projected results.

The company should inquire as to what extent the venture capitalist firm has available funds and whether it can provide additional expansion financing if needed. References from prior investees should be sought to ascertain the degree that the venture capitalist gets involved in operations and how it reacts when operations do not go so well.

Chapter Eight

Accounting Issues

ENTREPRENEUR'S OVERVIEW

The SEC has the authority under federal securities law to pre-scribe the accounting principles used and the form and the con-tent of financial statements filed with it. The SEC, however, has relied principally on standard-setting bodies established by the accounting profession. In the private sector, the Financial Ac-counting Standards Board (FASB) establishes the accounting principles for nongovernmental entities. In the absence of a pro-nouncement from FASB (or its predecessors), the American In-stitute of Certified Public Accountants, through its Accounting Standards Executive Committee (ACSEC), issues pronounce-ments that represent a source of established accounting principles.

The SEC staff stays abreast of the development of new ac-counting standards and influences the resulting standards. Often, it is the SEC that provides the impetus for a new standard from the private sector. The need for new standards frequently results from changes in the business and economic climate.

Either because the SEC is not satisfied with the interpretations that accounting practice has given to an accounting standard or because a standard does not exist for a variation or type of a fi-nancial transaction, the SEC may publish its own rules or inter-pretations. Because of the number of variations in circumstances that sometimes exist, there are accounting treatments preferred by the SEC staff that have not been published. The SEC will at times announce its preference on an issue at an open meeting of the Emerging Issues Task Force (EITF). These views are published as part of the EITF abstracts, which summarize the EITF proceedings. The EITF was established by the FASB and includes representatives of CPA firms and representatives of major associations of preparers of financial statements. It was created to respond to new issues on a timely basis within the framework of established accounting rules and practices. The SEC has indicated that it would challenge any accounting that differs from an EITF consensus.

An accounting treatment that is questioned and ultimately held to be in error by the SEC can severely alter a company's financial results. For a company in the middle of an IPO, it may, at best, result in a delayed offering and additional costs. At worst, it can lead to an abandoned offering, the loss of costs incurred, and the waste of management's energy and time. Consideration must also be given to whether it is appropriate to restate prior years' financial statements issued to creditors and private investors. A restatement has the potential to result in a violation of loan covenants, litigation, and a loss of confidence in the company by investors and lenders. For a company that is already public, the restatement of prior years' financials will probably result in a drop in market price, litigation, and the loss of market confidence. The monetary consequences can be severe if there has been an intervening public offering between the date the accounting treatment was adopted and the date it was held to be wrong. In addition, egregious errors can lead to SEC enforcement actions.

A review of significant sensitive or complex accounting areas before filing with the SEC is prudent. Consideration should be given to clearing these issues with the SEC where the answer is ambiguous. A request for the SEC staff's concurrence with the company's position should be made in writing, usually after an explanatory telephone call. A follow-up meeting with the staff may be necessary. The company's independent auditors often coordinate and usually participate in the interaction with the SEC.

A discussion of certain of the special or sensitive accounting issues follows.

BUSINESS COMBINATIONS

Poolings or Purchases

There are two basic methods to account for the merger of two or more entities. One method is called the pooling of interests method, and the other is called the purchase method. Specific criteria provide the means of identifying which method is the appropriate one. The rules are not designed to allow for a free choice as to what method must be used in a given transaction. Depending on the facts and circumstances, one of the methods is the correct one and must be the method used. The financial statement differences between the two methods can be huge. Since 1970, when the basic criteria now in use were established, there have been new variations in the form or conditions of merger transactions. In response, many new accounting interpretations have been made by both the SEC (including unpublished ones) and the private sector. The result is a labyrinth of rules.

The pooling of interests method is intended to reflect a combination of two or more previously independent businesses that combine as one and jointly share future risks. None of the businesses are considered as having acquired the other. Prior years' financial statements are combined as if the companies had been together from their inceptions. Equity of the combining companies are added together. Assets and liabilities are recorded by the combined entity at the same values as they had been on the separate accounts of each of the combining companies.

As indicated, if the specific criteria for a pooling are not met, the combination is accounted for as the acquisition of one entity by another and thus the purchase method is employed. Under the purchase method, the acquiring company records the acquisition, not at the values previously recorded by the acquired entity, but at the acquiring company's cost to purchase, which represents the fair value of the acquired company at the date of acquisition. The cost to acquire is allocated to the individual assets acquired and liabilities assumed at amounts equal to their fair values at date of acquisition. An excess of cost to acquire over the fair market value of the specifically identifiable net assets acquired is recorded as goodwill; an excess of fair market value of net assets acquired over cost to acquire results in negative goodwill.

Among the multiple criteria to determine if a merger qualifies as a pooling is that voting common stock must be exchanged for substantially all (at least 90 percent) of the voting common of another enterprise or exchanged for all the net assets of the other enterprise. Stock is also frequently used as part or all of the price in a transaction where purchase accounting is the appropriate method (i.e., one or more of the criteria for qualification as a pooling have failed). When purchase accounting is used and stock is issued to acquire a business, additional equity is created when the cost of the acquisition exceeds the recorded values of the acquired entity. Cost is the fair value of the stock issued or the fair value of the property received, whichever is the more evident. In a pooling, no additional equity is created. In periods after the acquisition, the purchase method, where the cost to acquire exceeds the value recorded by the acquired enterprise, results in higher charges to earnings than under the poolings method. When stock is used, if the immediate goal is the creation of equity, a purchase is wanted. If the goal is to avoid charges to future earnings, a pooling is wanted. The difference in accounting between the pooling and purchase methods can be so significant that some merger negotiations have foundered because of an inability to meet the criteria for a pooling.

Reverse Acquisition

When stock is used in a business combination accounted for as a purchase, the company that issues the stock is usually the acquirer. The assets of the acquired company are recorded at fair market value, with goodwill normally resulting. At times, however, the shareholders of the company being legally acquired wind up with voting and management control of the issuing company. In these situations, the legally acquired company is considered to be the acquirer from an accounting point of view. The assets of the issuing company, the legal acquirer, are revalued instead of the assets of the legally acquired company.

If cost is determined based on the fair value of the issuer's net assets rather than the fair market value of its stock, because the issuer is not a public company, goodwill does not result. When the issuer is not an operating company but a public shell, the acquisition is valued at the issuer's net tangible assets, and no goodwill results.

The prior year historical financial statements are those of the "accounting acquirer," although they are labeled as those of the issuer.

Predecessors

For accounting purposes, an acquired company is considered to be a predecessor by the SEC, either when it was owned by the successor's (acquirer's) controlling shareholders or when a non-operating company, whose assets consist mostly of cash, acquires an operating business from an unrelated party. The first transaction is accounted for as a pooling (companies under common control), and the second is accounted for as a purchase. However, whenever financial statements of the successor for years prior to the acquisition are included in a registration statement or annual report, the transactions of the predecessor must be included not only for pooling but also for purchase combinations.

GOODWILL, SPECIFICALLY IDENTIFIABLE INTANGIBLE ASSETS, AND AMORTIZATION THEREOF

Goodwill

As indicated, an excess of the cost to acquire a business that is accounted for under the purchase method over the fair market value of the specifically identifiable net assets acquired is recorded as goodwill; an excess of the fair market value of the specifically identifiable net assets acquired over the cost to acquire is recorded as negative goodwill. Generally, accepted accounting principles require that goodwill be amortized over a period not to exceed 40 years. The SEC will challenge lengthy amortization periods, especially where one of the following conditions exist for an acquired company: (1) it is not a mature company, (2) it is dependent on a few products or customers, (3) there is a high risk of product obsolescence, or (4) the industry is highly competitive. An acceptable amortization period of goodwill resulting from the acquisition of a high-tech company is in a five- to seven-year range.

Negative goodwill first reduces proportionately the values assigned to noncurrent assets other than long-term investments in marketable securities. After these noncurrent assets are reduced to zero, the remainder of the negative goodwill is classified as a deferred credit and amortized to income over the period to be benefited. Many acquiring companies believe that the circumstances surrounding an acquisition for less than fair market value indicate that the benefits are realized over a short term with a resulting increase to income over a few years. The SEC, however, will usually object to a 10-year or less amortization period for negative goodwill.

Specifically Identifiable Intangibles

Generally accepted accounting principles require that intangible assets that can be specifically identified, such as customer lists and licenses, should be valued separately in a business combination accounted for as a purchase. The SEC staff feels that, in order to obtain a longer amortization period, acquiring companies are remiss in not identifying such specific intangibles that are usually amortized over a shorter period than goodwill.

The SEC staff also perceives a general failure to allocate goodwill to acquired segments, lines of businesses, and separate business operations. As a result, there may be a failure to include goodwill as part of the cost of assets sold when a unit of an acquired business is subsequently sold. Failure to allocate to separate units or lines of business also makes it difficult to evaluate goodwill impairment.

Goodwill Impairment

The SEC staff's position is that the carrying amount of goodwill should be reduced if it is probable that the estimated undiscounted operating income from the related operations will be less than the carrying amount of the goodwill. Impairment measurement that uses discounted operating income or cash flows is acceptable to the staff. This is similar to the approach used in a Statement of Financial Accounting Standards issued for public comment by the FASB in March 1994. The method used to periodically measure and recognize the impairment of goodwill should be disclosed. In order to satisfy the SEC that write-downs were objectively made on a timely basis, entities should be able to prove that a consistent accounting policy has been applied and that events or objective evidence demonstrate a change in circumstances to support the write-down in the current period. Financial statement disclosures would include information such as reasons for the write-down, the events or changes in circumstances that led to the write-down, and how the amount of the write-down was determined.

CONTINGENT LIABILITIES ASSUMED BY THE PURCHASER IN A BUSINESS COMBINATION

The effect on the financial statements can be significant if a contingent liability of the acquired entity assumed in a purchase business combination cannot be reasonably estimated within a one-year period of the purchase.

A contingent liability is recorded when it is probable that a loss has occurred and the amount can be reasonably estimated. A contingent liability that does not meet such criteria until after one year of the acquisition will result in a charge to earnings in the period when the liability is finally accruable. On the other hand, if the liability can be estimated and accrued as part of the acquisition purchase price, the cost of the purchase is increased, with a resulting increase in the cost of the assets acquired. Frequently, the increase in acquisition cost is reflected as an increase in goodwill or other long-term asset. The cost attributed to the settlement of the contingent liability is thus charged to earnings over a longer period and not charged off in one year.

If contingent liabilities assumed by a purchaser in a business combination cannot be determined at the date of the acquisition, the acquiring company should disclose in its notes to financial statements that the purchase price allocation is preliminary. Disclosure should include the nature of the contingency and information that will enable a reader to understand its potential effects on the final allocation and on postacquisition operating results. Management's discussion and analysis should disclose the likely effects on operating results, liquidity, and financial condition.

If the acquiring company believes that it will take longer than one year to gather the information needed to make an allocation, the SEC encourages registrants to discuss the circumstances with the SEC staff. The one-year period will probably not be extended if it is unlikely that the liability can be estimated on the basis of information known to be obtainable at the time of the initial allocation of the purchase price.

DISCONTINUED OPERATIONS

The operations of and the gain or loss, net of taxes, from the disposal of a business segment are shown separately in the financial statements after income from continuing operations and before extraordinary items, if any. A segment refers to a component that represents a separate major line of business or class of customers. Reclassification of the operations as discontinued and recording the loss from disposal occurs on the date (referred to as the measurement date) management commits itself to a formal plan to dispose of a segment of the business. The SEC has recently published its views with regard to several issues in this area. Some of these SEC views are:

- A plan to dispose of a segment does not qualify for presentation of the segment as discontinued if management has not determined the particular method of disposition (i.e., sale, spin-off, or liquidation).

- A segment should not be reported as a discontinued operation unless the disposition of all the components of that segment is likely to be completed within a year of the measurement date.
- An orderly liquidation of a segment over a period that exceeds one year may be reported as a discontinued operation provided that the company ceases accepting new business (other than that which it is obligated by contract or regulation to accept) within 12 months of the measurement date and that the results of operations through final termination of the business can be estimated with reasonably accuracy.
- The results of operations of a segment of a business that has been sold should not be reported as discontinued operations if the company retains significant influence over its operations through minority ownership.
- Subsidiaries intended for disposal that do not satisfy the criteria for presentation as discontinued operations should continue to be consolidated unless matters outside the control of the company indicate that control does not rest presently with the company or is likely to be lost as a result of events outside the company's control.
- Management's discussion and analysis (MD&A) should include disclosure of known trends, events, and uncertainties involving discontinued operations that may materially affect the company's liquidity, financial condition, and results of operations between the measurement date for accounting purposes and the date when the material risks of those operations will be transferred or otherwise terminated. Contingent liabilities, such as product or environmental liabilities, that may remain with the registrant, notwithstanding disposal of the underlying business, should be disclosed in the financial statements and discussed in the MD&A.

ENVIRONMENTAL AND PRODUCT LIABILITIES

Many companies are contingently liable for damages arising from their products, the clean-up and reclamation of hazardous waste sites, and litigation costs. In most cases, these companies have claims for recovery from insurance carriers or other third parties. The accounting rules state that an estimated loss from a contingency shall be accrued and charged to income if it is probable that a liability has been incurred and the amount of the loss can be reasonably estimated. A claim for recovery reducing the loss should be recorded only when that claim is probable of realization. The rules also generally prohibit the offsetting of assets and liabilities unless each of two parties owes the other determinable amounts and the entity issuing financial statements has the right, enforceable at law, and intends to set off the amount owed with the amount owed to it by the other party.

However, determining the amount of the liability for environmental costs and amounts due from other Potentially Responsible Parties (PRPs), other parties (not named as PRPs), and insurance carriers may take years and involve protracted litigation. The extent of disclosure of the potential effect of the uncertainties on the future has varied. The timing of when costs and recoveries are recorded have also varied. In addition, assets for recoveries have been generally set off against liabilities for costs, although not always apparently offsettable within the accounting rules.

The differences in practice and the increasing magnitude of potential claims have caused the SEC staff to publish additional guidelines, among which are the following:

- The liability and the probable recovery should be presented separately on the face of the balance sheet.
- There is a rebuttable presumption that no asset should be recognized for a claim for recovery from a party that contends that it is not liable to indemnify the registrant. Registrants that overcome that presumption should

disclose the amount of recorded recoveries that are being contested and discuss the reasons for concluding that the amounts are probable of recovery.

- Discounting of environmental liabilities is appropriate only when the aggregate obligation and the amount and timing of the payments are fixed or reliably determinable. An estimate that represents the minimum in a range of equally likely outcomes does not qualify for discounting. The appropriate discount rate is the rate at which the liability could be settled in an arm's-length transaction. If that rate is not readily determinable, the rate should not exceed the interest rate on risk-free monetary assets having maturities comparable to that of the liability.
- Management may not delay loss accrual until only a single amount can be reasonably estimated. If management is able to determine that the amount of the liability is likely to fall within a range and no amount within the range can be determined to be the better estimate, the minimum amount of the range should be recorded.
- The company should accrue the estimated additional costs it will be required to pay if it is probable that another entity will not fully pay its allocated share of the costs.
- Extensive disclosures, in addition to the above, are required to provide an understanding of uncertainties affecting the measurement of the liability and the realization of assets.

REVENUE AND LOSS RECOGNITION

Revenue recognition or delayed loss recognition, often involving end-of-period transactions, are frequently a cause of SEC staff challenges to the financial statements filed. Two of the problem areas are bill and hold sales and barter transactions.

Bill and Hold Sales

Bill and hold transactions occur when the merchandise is not delivered but the sale is billed to the customer and included in revenue. The SEC has enumerated the following conditions that a bill and hold transaction should meet before revenues are recorded:

1. The risks of ownership must have passed to the buyer.
2. The customer must have made a fixed commitment to purchase the goods, preferably reflected in written documentation.
3. The buyer, not the seller, must request that the transaction be on a bill and hold basis. The buyer must have a substantial business purpose for ordering the goods on a bill and hold basis.
4. There must be a fixed schedule for delivery of the goods. The date for delivery must be reasonable and must be consistent with the buyer's business purpose (e.g., storage periods are customary in the industry).
5. The seller must not have retained any specific performance obligations such that the earnings process is not complete.
6. The ordered goods must have been segregated from the seller's inventory and not be subject to being used to fill other orders.
7. The equipment must be complete and ready for shipment.

The SEC further indicated that the above is not intended as a checklist. In some circumstances, a transaction may meet all the factors listed above but not meet the requirements for revenue recognition. In applying the above factors, the following should also be considered:

1. The date by which the seller expects payment, and whether it has modified its normal billing and credit terms for this buyer.
2. The seller's past experiences with and pattern of bill and hold transactions.
3. Whether the buyer has the expected risk of loss in the event of a decline in the market value of the goods.
4. Whether the seller's custodial risks are insurable and insured.

5. Whether APB Opinion No. 21, pertaining to the need for discounting the related receivable, is applicable.
6. Whether extended procedures are necessary in order to assure that there are no exceptions to the buyer's commitment to accept and pay for the goods sold (i.e., that the business reasons for the bill and hold have not introduced a contingency to the buyer's commitment).

As a result of these stringent criteria, a company will seldom be able to record revenue before shipment.

Barter Transactions

In a typical barter transaction, inventory is exchanged through a media-buying agency or barter company for future advertising credits with a rated value equal to the cost of the inventory. The cost of the inventory exchanged is transferred to prepaid advertising. The advertising credits in many such transactions, when exercised, can only be applied up to a stipulated percentage of the advertising bought with the balance (sometimes 50 percent) paid in cash.

The media-buying agency or barter company will often sell the inventory below the registrant's cost and obtain a discount below the rated value of the advertising credits. The company bartering the inventory will often allow much of the advertising credits to expire unused. The SEC has challenged barter transactions where the circumstances indicate a delayed write-off or write-down of inventory and has referred the issue to the Emerging Issues Task Force. The EITF, in early 1994 (Issue 93–11), reached a consensus that:

• Impairment of the nonmonetary asset exchanged (e.g., inventory or contractual rights such as operating leases) should be recognized before recording the exchange. The impairment is equal to the amount that the carrying amount of the nonmonetary asset exceeds its fair value. (Fair value in this case is defined as the amount that could reasonably be expected on a sale between a willing buyer and seller, other than in a forced sale or liquidation.) Fair value should not be based on an estimate of the value of the barter credits to be received. It would take persuasive evidence that fair value is higher than the carrying amount of the asset exchanged.

- The exchange for barter credits should then be reported at the fair value of the nonmonetary asset, unless there is a history of converting the barter credits to cash shortly after receiving them or if independent quoted market prices exist for items to be received upon exchange of the barter credits.

High-Technology Industries

Revenue recognition should be given careful scrutiny in any of the following circumstances:

- The customer has the right to return or exchange the product.
- Required installation has not been completed.
- Performance standards have yet to be met.
- Extended or special terms for payment exist.
- Sales are based on terms that protect the buyer should the buyer be unable to find a customer.

The SEC staff has recently addressed the following software recognition issues:

- Multiple product arrangements, if one or more products are not deliverable at inception of an agreement.
- Revenue recognition before a contract is signed.
- Determination of whether minimum royalty arrangements constitute fixed fee arrangements.
- Contract segmentation.

DEFERRED CHARGES

Advertising

The Accounting Standards Executive Committee of the AICPA has a project to study the appropriateness of deferring costs, such as advertising, preoperating, and start-up costs. The first cost studied was advertising. The conclusion reached is that advertising will be expensed as incurred or not later than the first time the advertising has taken place. Only the incremental costs incurred in direct response advertising that is expected to result in probable future benefits can be deferred. A proven track record and supporting documentation of the responses are required to support the deferred advertising. Allocated administrative costs, depreciation, and other occupancy costs are not deferrable. Only direct incremental costs incurred in transactions with third parties and payroll and payroll-related costs directly related to direct response advertising are deferrable.

Start-Up and Preoperating Costs

The SEC staff has expressed the following views concerning start-up and preoperating costs, which the staff categorizes as soft costs:

- Expensing preoperating costs immediately is almost always the preferred accounting method. It is therefore very difficult to justify an accounting change to, or the adoption by a new entity of, a policy to capitalize preoperating costs.
- Only direct incremental costs incurred prior to operations may be capitalized as start-up costs. The amortization period should not exceed one or two years.
- Interest and depreciation should not be part of deferred start-up or preoperating costs.
- Capitalization of start-up costs must cease when operations begin, rather than upon achieving a predetermined percent of capacity.

SPECIAL PURPOSE ENTITIES

Beginning in 1989, the SEC staff indicated that it was becoming concerned with transactions involving what the SEC referred to as Special Purpose Entities (SPEs). These are entities that lack substance but that enter into transactions with registrants for the purpose of affecting how a transaction is reflected by a registrant.

The SPE, for example, may be a lessor that holds title to a property, but the public lessee assumes substantially all of the risks and rewards of ownership. The objective might be to avoid the capitalization of the lease and obtain operating lease accounting treatment.

The EITF in Issue No. 90–15 dealt with the subject of leasing transactions involving SPEs. The EITF, in their consensus, concluded that a lessee is required to consolidate a special-purpose entity lessor when all of the following conditions exist:

1. Substantially all of the activities of the SPE involve assets that are to be leased to a single lessee.
2. The expected substantive residual risks and substantially all of the residual rewards of the leased asset(s) and the obligation imposed by the underlying debt of the SPE reside directly or indirectly with the lessee through such means as, for example:
   a. The lease agreement.
   b. A residual value guarantee through, for example, the assumption of first dollar of loss provisions.
   c. A guarantee of the SPE's debt.
   d. An option granting the lessee a right to (1) purchase the leased asset at a fixed price or at a defined price other than fair value determined at the date of exercise or (2) receive any of the lessor's sales proceeds in excess of a stipulated amount.
3. The owner(s) of record of the SPE has not made an initial substantive residual equity capital investment that is at risk during the entire term of the lease.

The SEC staff has indicated that it expects to resolve other transactions on a case-by-case basis and that the conditions set forth in Issue 90–75 may be useful in evaluating other types of transactions between SPEs and registrants.

PRO FORMA INFORMATION

Pro forma financial data and pro forma financial statements give effect to significant transactions that are not reflected, or only partially reflected, in the historic financial statements. The significant transactions included on a pro forma basis are ones that are probable of occurring, or occur, after the balance sheet date, such as the purchase of a business. Other pro forma adjustments may arise from transactions that have occurred prior to the balance sheet date but the effect has not been included as part of operations for a full fiscal year. An example of the latter is the purchase of a business in the middle of the year.

Pro forma data are included when the information is considered material to a lender or investor. It is often a matter of judgment as to whether pro forma information is necessary. However, generally accepted accounting principles require pro forma data in certain circumstances. Examples of pro forma data required by generally accepted accounting principles are:

- Disclosure by public companies in the notes to financial statements, for the period in which it acquires a business accounted for as a purchase, of the pro forma results of operations for: (1) the current period, as though the combination had taken place at the beginning of the period; and (2) the immediately preceding period, as though the combination had taken place at the beginning of that period.
- For accounting changes that are not reflected retroactively as adjustments of prior years' statements, pro forma income before extraordinary items, net income, and earnings per share for these two captions should be shown for all periods presented as if the newly adopted accounting principle had been adopted in those years.
- Effects of significant events occurring subsequent to the balance sheet date.

The SEC has more extensive requirements. The SEC requirements are set forth in the various registration or reporting forms (e.g., Forms S-1, SB-1, SB-2, Form 8-K), Regulation S-X (Form and Content of and Requirements for Financial Statements), and Staff Accounting Bulletins. Some requirements are based on SEC staff practice.

The format for presentation of pro forma information varies. A significant business combination or disposition usually requires pro forma combined (or combining) statements. In certain cases, the pro forma results are required by the SEC to be presented on the face of the historic income statement (an example is reflecting pro forma income taxes on the face for years when the registrant functioned as a Subchapter S corporation). At other times, judgment may dictate as to whether, for example, a pro forma balance sheet should be displayed alongside the historic balance sheet or whether disclosing pro forma information in the notes to the financial statements is sufficient.

Pro forma data must also be reflected in the summary and selected financial information sections of the prospectus.

Significant Business Combinations and Pro Forma Information

The extensive SEC requirements for pro forma data when a significant business combination has occurred or is probable are outlined in Article 11 of Regulation S-X.

A combination is significant for purposes of determining if pro forma financial information is required if any of the following three comparisons, using data from the preacquisition annual statements of the registrant and the acquired business, exceeds 10 percent.

1. In a combination accounted for as a purchase, compare the registrant's investment in (or consideration paid for) the acquiree to the registrant's consolidated assets. Contingent consideration should be considered as part of the total investment in the acquiree unless its payment is deemed remote. In a pooling, compare the number of shares exchanged to the registrant's outstanding shares immediately before combination.

2. Compare the registrant's share of the acquired entity's total assets to the registrant's consolidated assets.

3. Compare the registrant's equity in the acquired entity's income from continuing operations before taxes to that of the registrant.

    If the registrant's income for the most recent fiscal year is 10 percent or more lower than the average of the last five fiscal years, the average income of the registrant may be used for this computation. Loss years should be assigned a value of zero in computing the numerator for this average, but the denominator stays at five. This alternate computation is not applicable if the registrant reported a loss, rather than income, in the latest fiscal year. The acquiree's income may not be averaged pursuant to this rule.

Where the test involves combined entities, entities reporting losses shall not be aggregated with entities reporting income.

If a significant business combination has occurred in the latest fiscal year or subsequent thereto, or is probable, a pro forma condensed balance sheet as of the date of the most recent historic balance sheet of the registrant included in the filing should be included. A pro forma balance sheet is not required if the acquisition is already reflected in the historic balance sheet. A pro forma condensed income statement for both the latest fiscal year and interim period should be included in the filing, unless the historic income statement reflects the transaction for the entire period. If the business combination is to be accounted for as a pooling of interests that has not occurred prior to the latest balance sheet presented, pro forma combined income statements shall be filed for all periods for which historic income statements of the registrant are required. A financial forecast may be presented in lieu of a pro forma statement of operations. The use of forecasts has been rare.

Pro forma adjustments for the balance sheet should give effect to events that: (1) are directly attributable to the transaction, (2) are factually supportable, (3) have a continuing impact, and (4) are nonrecurring. They are computed as if the transaction was consummated on the balance sheet date.

Pro forma adjustments for income statements:

- Should be computed assuming the transaction occurred at the beginning of the fiscal year presented and should be carried forward through any interim period presented.

- Should give effect to events that are directly attributable to the transaction, factually supportable, and expected to have a continuing impact.
- Should not include material nonrecurring charges or credits and related tax effects that result directly from the transaction and that will be included in the income of the registrant within the 12 months succeeding the transaction. A note should disclose those items and clearly indicate that they were not included.
- Should not eliminate infrequent or nonrecurring items that are included in the underlying historical financial statements and are not directly affected by the transaction.

The following should also be observed in preparing pro forma income statements:

- Where the registrant has adopted a change in accounting principle, the pro forma information should consistently apply the newly adopted accounting principle to all periods presented.
- Tax effects normally should be calculated with reference to the statutory rate in effect during the periods for which the pro forma income statements are presented.
- The historical statement of income used in pro forma presentations should not report discontinued operations, extraordinary items, or the cumulative effect of accounting changes. If the historical statements include these items, only the portion of the income statement through income from continuing operations should be presented.
- Historical primary and fully diluted per share data based on continuing operations and pro forma primary and fully diluted per share data should be presented on the face of the pro forma statements of operations.
- When a business combination is accounted for as a pooling, the computation of earnings per share should be based on the aggregate of the weighted average outstanding shares of the constituent businesses, adjusted to equivalent shares of the surviving business for all

periods presented. The computation of earnings per share for a combination of entities under common control should be similar with historical EPS adjusted for any "cheap stock" issuances.

- An acquired entity's income statement should be brought up to within 93 days of the registrant's fiscal year, if practicable, by adding subsequent interim results to the fiscal year's data and deducting the comparable preceding year interim results, with appropriate disclosure.

The pro forma financial statements should be presented in columnar form, with separate columns presenting historical results, pro forma adjustments, and pro forma results. The statements should be preceded by an introductory paragraph that briefly describes the transaction, the entities involved, the periods presented, and an explanation of what the pro forma presentation shows. Generally, pro forma adjustments should be presented gross on the face of the pro forma statements unless net presentations are reconciled in the notes to the pro forma statements. The adjustments should be referenced to footnotes that clearly explain the assumptions involved. Pro forma information should be in condensed form.

If the transaction is structured in such a manner that significantly different results may occur, additional pro forma presentations should be made that give effect to the range of possible results. When consummation of more than one transaction has occurred or is probable, pro forma information may be presented on a combined basis, with footnote explanations of the various transactions and maximum variances possible. However, it may be more useful to present the information on a disaggregated basis. In business combinations accounted for as a purchase, typical pro forma adjustments would include allocation of the purchase price, adjusting assets and liabilities to fair value, and recognizing intangibles and acquisition-related liabilities.

If the registrant is awaiting additional information necessary for the measurement of a contingency of the acquired company, the registrant should disclose that the purchase price allocation is preliminary. In this circumstance, the registrant should describe the nature of the contingency and furnish other available information that will enable the reader to understand the magnitude of any potential accrual and the range of reasonably possible loss.

If contingent consideration is issuable based on future earnings, the registrant should disclose the terms of the contingent consideration and the potential impact on future earnings. If amortization of purchase adjustments is not straight-line, the effect on operating results for the five years following the acquisition should be disclosed in a note, if material. A schedule showing the calculation of the purchase price (including the value assigned to noncash portions) should be provided in a note, if not otherwise evident.

Other Pro Forma Presentations

Subchapter S Corporations and Partnerships. If the company was formerly a Subchapter S corporation, partnership, or similar tax pass-through enterprise, pro forma tax and earnings per share data should be presented on the face of historical statements as follows:

- If necessary pro forma adjustments to earnings include more than adjustments for taxes, limit the pro forma presentation to the latest year and the interim period.
- If necessary adjustments include only taxes, a pro forma earnings per share presentation of all periods presented is encouraged, but not required.
- Historical earnings per share data should not be presented.

In filings for periods subsequent to becoming taxable, pro forma presentations reflecting tax expense for earlier comparable periods should continue to calculate the pro forma tax expense based on statutory rates in effect for the earlier period.

Undistributed earnings or losses of a Subchapter S corporation should be reclassified to paid-in capital upon termination of the election.

Subchapter S corporations or partnerships that pay distributions to the promoter-owner with proceeds from the offering should follow the pro forma presentations specified in the following section.

Distributions to Promoters-Owners at or prior to Closing of an IPO. If a planned distribution to owners subsequent to the balance sheet date is not given retroactive effect in the latest balance sheet, but would be significant in relation to reported equity, a pro forma balance sheet reflecting the distribution (but not giving effect to the offering proceeds) should be presented alongside the historical balance sheet in the filing.

If a distribution to owners (whether already reflected in the balance sheet or not, whether declared or not) is to be paid out of proceeds of the offering rather than from the current year's earnings, historical per share data should be deleted and pro forma per share data should be presented (for the latest year and interim period only), giving effect to the number of shares whose proceeds would be necessary to pay the dividend. A dividend declared in the latest year would be deemed to be in contemplation of the offering with the intention of repayment out of offering proceeds to the extent that the dividend exceeded earnings during the previous 12 months.

Other Changes in Capitalization at or prior to Closing of IPO. A registrant may elect to present retroactively a conversion of securities as if it had occurred at the date of the latest balance sheet included in the filing with no adjustment of earlier statements. However, if the original instrument accrues interest or accretes toward redemption value after the balance sheet date until the conversion actually occurs, or if the terms of the conversion do not confirm the carrying value, only a pro forma presentation would be deemed appropriate.

If terms of outstanding equity securities will change subsequent to the date of the latest balance sheet and the new terms result in a material reduction of permanent equity or, if redemption of a material amount of equity securities will occur in conjunction with the offering, the filing should include a pro forma balance sheet (excluding effects of offering proceeds), presented alongside the historical balance sheet, giving effect to the change in capitalization.

If the conversion of outstanding securities will occur subsequent to the latest balance sheet date and the conversion will result in a material reduction of earnings applicable to common shareholders (excluding effects of the offering), the staff will not object to the deletion (or inclusion solely in the notes to the financial statements) of historical earnings per share, if such information is deemed irrelevant. Pro forma earnings per share for the latest year and interim period should be presented, giving effect to the conversion (but not the offering).

Carve-Outs. In an initial public offering, if a registrant has operated as a subsidiary, division, or lesser business component of another entity, pro forma adjustments are required to:

- Reflect expenses incurred on behalf of the registrant that were not charged to it. The historic statements would include an allocation of uncharged expenses on a reasonable basis. An explanation of the method of allocation would be included in the notes to the financial statements. However, if interest has not been charged on intercompany debt, extensive disclosure rather than a charge for interest is required.
- The latest year-end and interim period would reflect pro forma income tax provisions calculated on a separate return basis.
- Provide pro forma income statements to reflect revised or terminated tax or cost-sharing agreements. Historical earnings per share should not be shown on the historical income statements. Only pro forma earnings per share for the most recent year and interim period should be shown.
- Dividends declared by a subsidiary after the balance sheet date will either be given retroactive effect or reflected in a

pro forma balance sheet. When dividends are paid from the proceeds of the offering or when the dividends exceed earnings in the current year, historical earnings per share are not shown and only pro forma per share data for the latest year and interim period are shown. Pro forma per share data should give effect to the increase in the number of shares that, when multiplied by the offering price, would have been sufficient to replace the capital in excess of earnings being withdrawn.

Salary Adjustments. Executive salaries of closely held companies are at times substantially reduced by new employment contracts that will take effect after the public offering. The new contracts often arise as a result of a merger. Retroactive adjustments to reduce salary expense are not appropriate. However, the financial statements may be supplemented with a pro forma financial presentation that shows the effects of salary changes that are supported by employment agreements. Such a pro forma presentation should be limited to the latest fiscal year and any subsequent interim period presented.

Inclusion of Offering Proceeds on a Pro Forma Basis. Pro forma financial statements may not reflect the receipt or application of offering proceeds, except as follows:

- To the extent of a firm commitment from the underwriter.
- To the extent of the minimum in a best-efforts minimum/maximum offering.
- In a best-efforts all-or-none offering.

Certain exceptions also exist for savings and loan conversions.

A similar prohibition may apply to capitalization tables, except that presentation at both minimum and maximum in a minimum/maximum offering is acceptable.

Other. Other transactions that require pro forma financial statements are:

- Disposition of a significant portion of a business, either by sale, abandonment, or distribution to shareholders, has occurred or is probable and is not fully reflected in the historical financial statements.
- Acquisition of one or more real estate operations that are in the aggregate significant has occurred in the latest fiscal year or subsequent interim period, or is probable.
- Roll-up of partnerships (see Regulation S-K, Standard Instructions for Filing Forms under Securities Act of 1933, Securities Exchange Act of 1934, and Energy Policy and Conservation Act of 1975, Item 914).

EQUITY SECURITIES ISSUED WITHIN A ONE-YEAR PERIOD PRIOR TO FILING AN IPO

Earnings per Share

In computing earnings per share, stock and warrants issued within a one-year period prior to the initial filing of an IPO should be treated as outstanding for all reported periods. This is the same treatment accorded to shares issued in a stock split or a recapitalization effected contemporaneously with an IPO. The result is a decrease in earnings or loss per share. The additional shares are included in the earnings per share calculation, even if they are antidilutive.

Compensation

Stock, options, or warrants issued to employees, consultants, directors, or others providing services to the issuer within one year prior to the filing of an initial registration at a price (or exercise price) below the offering price are presumed to be compensatory.

In evaluating whether the stock issuance is, in fact, a compensation arrangement or a restructuring of ownership rights prior to the offering, the circumstances of the issuance and the extent of employee participation should be considered.

In determining the fair value of the stock, if compensatory, the registrant should consider the proximity of the issuance to the offering, intervening events, transfer restrictions and exercise dates, and profitability and the financial condition of the company. The SEC staff looks to objective evidence as the best support for the determination of market value. Examples of objective evidence include transactions with third parties involving issuances or repurchases of stock for cash and/or appraisals by reputable investment bankers independent of the offering at or near the issue date.

Transfers of Nonmonetary Assets

Transfers of nonmonetary assets to a company by its promoters (founders or organizers) or shareholders in exchange for stock prior to or at the time of the company's initial public offering should normally be recorded at the promoters' or shareholders' historical cost basis.

Accounting for Shares Placed in Escrow in Connection with an Initial Public Offering

In some initial public offerings, certain promoter/shareholder groups place some of their shares in escrow, with subsequent release of the shares contingent upon the registrant's attainment of certain goals, such as earnings. Although these shares are legally outstanding and are reported as such on the face of the balance sheet, the SEC staff considers the escrowed shares to be "contingent shares" for purposes of calculating earnings per share. The agreement to release the shares upon the achievement of the stipulated goal is presumed by the staff to be a separate compensatory arrangement between the registrant and the promoters. Accordingly, the fair value of the shares at the time they are released from escrow should be recognized as a charge to income in that period. No compensation expense need be recognized with respect to shares released to a person who has had no relationship to the registrant other than as a shareholder (for example, he or she is not an officer, director, employee, consultant, or contractor) and who is not expected to have any relationship other than as shareholder to the company in the future.

AUDITED FINANCIAL STATEMENTS OF ACQUIRED COMPANIES—SPECIAL RULE THAT MAY BE AVAILABLE FOR INITIAL PUBLIC OFFERINGS ON FORM S-1

Rule 3–05 of Regulation S-X requires a registrant to file audited financial statements of an acquired entity for one, two, or three years, depending upon the relative size of the entity acquired, using three tests specified in Rule 1–02(v) of Regulation S-X. The tests consist of the same comparisons used in determining a significant combination in the above discussion of pro forma requirements. The calculations are required to be based on the registrant's financial statements as they appear at the end of its last fiscal year and the acquired company's financial statements as they appear at the end of its last fiscal year.

The SEC has recognized that the tests may not be appropriate if applied to a first-time registrant with substantial growth in assets and earnings in recent years, primarily as a result of acquisitions. The significance of an acquired entity in this type of situation, it was felt, might be better measured in relation to the size of the registrant at the time the registration statement was filed, rather than its size at the time the acquisition was made. Therefore, for a first-time registrant, the three tests of Rule 1–02(v) are measured against the total entities, including those to be acquired, which comprise the registrant at the time the registration statement is filed, as follows:

1. For the registrant's most recent fiscal year, the financial statements of at least 90 percent of the total entities comprising the registrant must be audited. Separate audited financial statements would be required, for periods up to the date of acquisition, for each entity

acquired during the latest fiscal year of the registrant whose audited financial statements were necessary to meet the 90 percent test. Audited financial statements would also be required of entities proposed to be acquired if necessary to meet the 90 percent test along with appropriate pro forma financial statements.

2. For the year preceding the latest full fiscal year, audited financial statements are required for two full years for entities accounting for at least 80 percent of the total of the entities comprising, or that will comprise, the registrant. To the extent that the results of the entities constituting the 80 percent are not included in consolidated financial statements for two full years, audited financial statements of such entities must be filed that report on a consecutive time span of two years (including the period in the consolidated financial statements).

3. For year three, the earliest of the three years to be reported on, audited financial statements are required for three full years (years one, two, and three) only for entities accounting for at least 60 percent of the total of the entities comprising, or that will comprise, the registrant.

Application of this modification is limited to situations in which acquisitions of businesses and the subsequent operation thereof are in discrete distinguishable form, such that assets and revenues from each entity can be clearly and separately identified.

SEC Staff Accounting Bulletin 80 includes illustrative examples.

Appendix
SAMPLE PRO FORMA FINANCIAL STATEMENTS

Lilac Corp.
PRO FORMA FINANCIAL STATEMENTS

(unaudited)

The following unaudited pro forma combined balance sheet and statements of earnings have been prepared based on the historical financial statements of Lilac Corp. and Mint Inc. The pro forma combined balance sheet as of March 31, 1994, is presented as if the acquisition of Mint Inc. by Lilac Corp. and the completion of the public offering took place on March 31, 1994. The pro forma combined statements of operations for the periods ended December 31, 1993, and March 31, 1994, give effect to the acquisition as if such acquisition occurred on January 1, 1993. Pro forma adjustments and assumptions on which the pro forma financial statements are based are described in the notes to the pro forma combined financial statements. They are based on the assumption that the acquisition of Mint Inc. is accounted for under the purchase method of accounting.

The unaudited pro forma financial statements should be read in conjunction with the historical financial statements of the (Lilac Corp.) and Mint Inc. and the related notes thereto that are contained elsewhere in this prospectus.

The unaudited pro forma information does not purport to be indicative of what the company's financial position or results of operations would actually have been if such transactions, in fact, had occurred on those dates or to project the company's financial position or results of operations for any future date or period.

Lilac Corp.
PRO FORMA COMBINED BALANCE SHEET

As of March 31, 1994
(unaudited)

ASSETS	Lilac Corp. Historical	Mint Inc. Historical	Pro Forma Adjustments	Pro Forma Combined
		(in thousands)		
CURRENT ASSETS				
Cash	$ 900	$ 400	$ (300) (1)	$ 2,500
			4,500 (2)	
			(3,000) (3)	
Accounts receivable	3,000	1,600		4,600
Inventory	1,500	1,000		2,500
Total current assets	5,400	3,000	1,200	9,600
FIXED ASSETS (NET)	1,200	450		1,650
GOODWILL	700		900 (1)	1,600
OTHER ASSETS	100	50		150
Total assets	$7,400	$3,500	$2,100	$13,000
	LIABILITIES AND STOCKHOLDERS' EQUITY			
CURRENT LIABILITIES				
Accounts payable	$2,500	$1,600	$50 (1)	$4,150
Notes payable—banks	300	400		700
Accrued expenses	450	150		600
Income taxes payable	200	50		250
Current maturities of long-term debt	50	20		70
Total current liabilities	3,500	2,220	50	5,770
LONG-TERM DEBT	250	30		280
DEFERRED INCOME TAXES	50			50
Total liabilities	3,800	2,250	50	6,100
Total stockholders' equity	3,600	1,250	1,800 (1)	
			(1,250) (1)	
			4,500 (2)	
			(3,000) (3)	6,900
Total liabilities and stockholders' equity	$7,400	$3,500	$2,100	$13,000

Lilac Corp.
NOTES TO PRO FORMA COMBINED BALANCE SHEET

As of March 31, 1994
(unaudited)

(1) To record the adjustments resulting from the purchase of all of Mint Inc.'s stock for $2.1 million consisting of 300,000 shares of Lilac common stock at $6 per share and $300,000 of cash. Estimated acquisition costs of $50,000 are also reflected. The historical book value of the acquired identifiable assets approximate their respective fair market values. The excess of the purchase price over the fair value of the net identifiable assets acquired has been recorded as goodwill and will be amortized over 20 years.

200,000 shares of Lilac Corp. common stock at $6 a share	$1,800,000
Cash	300,000
Acquisition costs	50,000
Cost of acquisition	2,150,000
Less fair value of net identifiable assets acquired	1,250,000
Goodwill	$ 900,000

(2) To record the estimated proceeds from the initial public offering of 600,000 shares of common stock, assuming an initial public offering price of $9 per share, net of $900,000 estimated offering costs.

(3) To record the distribution to the original stockholders of the company of approximately $3 million representing the undistributed S corporation earnings of the company as of March 31, 1994.

Lilac Corp.
PRO FORMA COMBINED STATEMENT OF OPERATIONS

For the year ended December 31, 1993
(unaudited)

	Lilac Corp. Historical	Mint Inc. Historical	Pro Forma Adjustments	Pro Forma Combined
	(in thousands, except per share data)			
Net Sales	$18,000	$14,000		$32,000
Cost of goods sold	15,000	11,000		26,000
Gross profit	3,000	3,000		6,000
Selling and administrative expenses	1,200	2,500	$ 45 (1) (100) (2)	3,645
Income from operations	1,800	500	55	2,355
Interest expense	50	30		80
Earnings before provision for income taxes	1,750	470	55	2,275
Provision for income taxes		160	722 (3)	882
NET EARNINGS	$ 1,750	$ 310	$(667)	$ 1,393
Net earnings	$ 1,750			
Contractual salary reductions	100			
	1,850			
Income taxes	740			
Pro forma historical earnings	$ 1,110 (4)			
Pro forma earnings per share	$.79 (5)			$.87
Weighted average number of common shares used in computation	1,400,000			1,600,000

Lilac Corp.
PRO FORMA COMBINED STATEMENT OF OPERATIONS

For the three months ended March 31, 1994 (unaudited)

	Lilac Corp. Historical	Mint Inc. Historical	Pro Forma Adjustments	Pro Forma Combined
	(in thousands, except per share data)			
Net sales	$6,000	$3,500		$9,500
Cost of goods sold	5,000	2,600		7,600
Gross profit	1,000	900		1,900
Selling and administrative expenses	500	700	$11 (1) (25) (2)	1,186
Income from operations	500	200	14	714
Interest expense	12	7		19
Earnings before provision for income taxes	488	193	14	695
Provision for income taxes		68	201 (3)	269
NET EARNINGS	$ 488	$ 125	$(184)	$ 426
Net earnings	$488			
Contractual salary reductions	25			
	513			
Income taxes	205			
Pro forma historical earnings	$ 308 (4)			
Pro forma earnings per share	$.22 (5)			$.27
Weighted average number of common shares used in computation	1,400,000			1,600,000

Lilac Corp.
NOTES TO PRO FORMA COMBINED STATEMENTS OF OPERATIONS

For the year ended December 31, 1993, and the three months ended March 31, 1994
(unaudited)

(1) To record amortization of goodwill resulting from the acquisition of Mint Inc. over a 20-year period.

(2) To adjust officers' salaries to reflect the difference between existing compensation and compensation in accordance with agreements that will take effect upon consummation of the offering.

(3) As discussed in Note A, the Company has elected to be taxed as an S corporation pursuant to the Internal Revenue Code. As a result of the initial public offering, the Company will become subject to federal and additional state income taxes. The pro forma provision for income taxes represents the provision for income taxes based on pro forma pretax income that would have been reported had the Company been subject to federal and additional state income taxes.

(4) Pro forma historical earnings includes adjustments to the historical income statement data to reflect the contractual reduction in officers' salaries and to reflect income taxes on a basis as if the Company had not elected S corporation status.

(5) Pro forma historical net earnings per share reflects the estimated portion of shares being offered by the company (400,000 shares) necessary to fund the payment of undistributed taxable S corporation earnings to the Company's current stockholders upon the termination of the Company's status as an S corporation.

Glossary

acceleration (1) Waiver of the required waiting period, after filing, for a registration statement to become effective. For example, under the Securities Act of 1933, a registration statement is effective 20 days after filing. In order to permit orderly processing and prevent the registration from becoming automatically effective, the registration statement includes a delaying amendment. When the statement has been cleared with the SEC and the securities are ready to be sold, a pricing amendment is filed and acceleration is requested to prevent further delay.

(2) When the balance of a loan becomes immediately payable because the borrower defaults on repayment or fails to comply with the terms of other covenants in the loan agreement.

accredited investors Individuals and financial institutions to whom unregistered securities may be sold in a private placement under Regulation D. Criteria as to net worth or income required to qualify as an accredited investor are specified in Regulation D.

all-hands meetings Meetings in connection with a public offering or private placement that include company officers, company attorneys, representatives of the underwriter, underwriter's attorneys, and the auditors.

all-or-none underwriting See *best-efforts underwriting*.

audit of financial statements Process and procedures by which an independent auditor comes to a conclusion (expresses an opinion) as to whether specified financial statements are presented fairly, in all material respects, in conformity with generally accepted accounting principles or in conformity with another comprehensive basis of accounting.

balance sheet A financial statement that lists an enterprise's assets, liabilities, and equity as of a given date. Also referred to as a statement of financial position.

best-efforts underwriting The underwriters do not agree to purchase unsold shares. Best-efforts agreements will often specify that all the securities (all-or-none) or a stated minimum have to be sold or the money will be refunded to subscribers. See *firm commitment underwriting*.

blind pool offering Use of proceeds from the offering is not specifically known at the effective date.

blue sky laws State laws establishing rules for registration and sale of securities within the state where securities will be sold.

bond A security evidencing money borrowed and promising to repay specific sum(s) at specified dates.

book value Net equity or net worth (assets less liabilities) as recorded on the books of an enterprise. Can also refer to the amount of a specific asset or liability as recorded on the books of an enterprise. Generally not the equivalent of fair or market values.

capital (1) Funds raised by an enterprise from lenders or stockholders, (2) funds invested by the owners of a business, (3) net worth or stockholders' equity reflected on the balance sheet, (4) net worth plus long-term liabilities, and (5) assets with long-term use (capital assets), such as plant and property.

closing A meeting, about one week after the effective date, at which the registrant receives the proceeds from the offering in exchange for the stock.

comfort letter Letter from the independent auditors mostly describing procedures performed at the request of the underwriter on unaudited data appearing in the prospectus and the auditors' findings. The purpose is to assist the underwriters with their due diligence obligation.

common stock A class of capital stock that usually has the voting rights and, in the event of dissolution, the rights to the remaining assets after satisfaction of liabilities and senior equity securities, such as preferred stock.

convertible security A debt instrument or preferred stock that can be exchanged at the option of the holder for shares of common stock at a stated price per share.

corporation A legal entity whose existence is independent of its shareholders. The shareholders usually are not liable for corporate debts beyond the amount of their investment.

debenture An uncollateralized debt whose repayment is dependent on the general credit of the issuer.

derivative A contract whose value is derived from an underlying asset. Examples of derivatives are options or warrants to buy a security and currency futures. Interest swaps (contracts that exchange fixed rates of interest for fluctuating rates or vice versa) are also referred to as derivatives.

dilution (1) The amount paid for stock in excess of the net tangible book value, usually calculated on a per share basis; (2) potential reduction in earnings per share resulting from the exercise of options, warrants, convertible securities, or other contingent issuances of stock.

due diligence A "reasonable" investigation performed by a company's underwriter, attorney, independent accountants, and other experts. The purpose is to satisfy a requirement that at the effective date of a 1933 Act registration statement, there was no reason to believe that there were any material misstatements or omissions.

earnings per share The amount of net income earned on a share of common stock for a given time period (a year or less). The computation can be quite complex in order to reflect potential dilution that might result from convertible securities, options, warrants, or other contingent issuances of stock.

EDGAR The SEC's electronic data gathering, analysis, and retrieval system that enables companies to file by computer.

effective date The date on which sales of securities being registered can start.

filing date The date on which a registration statement or other report is received by the SEC.

firm commitment underwriting The underwriters agree to buy all the securities offered at a discount from the public offering price. See *best-efforts underwriting*.

float Shares of a company's stock held by the public. Excludes shares held by insiders.

going public The sale of stock to the general public by a closely held corporation.

insiders Generally, officers, directors, and holders of 10 percent or more are considered insiders.

interim financial statements Balance sheets prepared at a date other than a company's fiscal year-end and statements of earnings and cash flows for a period or periods covering less than a full fiscal year.

letter of comments A letter from the SEC staff containing questions, critiques, and requests for more information concerning a document filed with the SEC.

letter of intent A letter signed by the underwriter and the company planning to go public that covers the expected terms of underwriting. The letter is nonbinding except for the company's obligation to pay for certain expenses.

letter stock Stock with a legend printed on it stating that it is restricted as to its resale.

leverage Ratio of debt to equity. Highly leveraged refers to a company with a high ratio of debt to equity.

leveraged buyout (LBO) Acquisition of a business with a high portion of borrowed funds. Usually, the intent is to repay with cash generated by the acquired company and/or a public offering.

limited liability company Owned by members who are not personally liable for the company's letters. May also qualify for tax treatment as a partnership.

mortgage Long-term debt collateralized by a specific property.

partnership (1) A general partnership is a business operated by two or more people, called general partners, in an unincorporated form. The partners are usually personally liable for partnership liabilities; (2) a limited partnership is a partnership of one or more general partners and one or more limited partners. Limited partners may limit their personal liability for partnership debts to the amount of their investment. For income tax purposes, partnership income is "passed through" to the partners, who include the income on their tax returns.

preferred stock An equity security that is senior to common stock in that it usually has preference over common stock as to dividends and distributions in liquidation. Usually nonvoting. At times includes features such as rights to conversion to common, to redemption by a specified date, or to payment of dividends in arrears before dividends on common can be paid (cumulative dividends).

private placement Sale of securities (usually to a few investors) that is not a "public offering."

proxy Written permission given by a shareholder to another person to vote on the shareholder's behalf.

quiet period Period from the date the company and underwriter plan to issue stock until 90 days after offering is completed. During this period, the company is limited as to the types of public statements that it can make.

red herring Preliminary prospectus circulated prior to the effective date of the registration. Contains a legend (red herring) indicating that the registration is not yet effective, that the prospectus is subject to amendment, and that it does not constitute an offer to sell or a solicitation of an offer to buy.

road show Tour organized by underwriters, designed to provide information about the company to professional money managers.

short swing profits Profits made by an officer, director, or 10 percent owner on the purchase and sale, or sale and purchase, of equity securities within a six-month period. These profits are required to be turned over to the corporation.

statement of cash flows A financial statement that provides information about an enterprise's cash receipts and cash payments classified between operating activities, investing activities, and financing activities for a specified period.

statement of earnings A financial statement that summarizes an enterprise's revenues, expenses, gains, and losses for a specified period. The resulting net amount shown is the net earnings for the period. Frequently referred to as the income statement.

stop order Means by which trading or effectiveness of a registration statement is suspended by the SEC.

Subchapter S corporation A corporation that has made an election not to be subject to the corporate income tax. Instead, the stockholders are taxed on the corporation's income. An S corporation must meet certain criteria to qualify for this election.

tender Offer by one company to buy the stock of another at a stated price. Can also refer to an offer made by a company for its own securities.

underwriter Investment banker or broker who agrees to purchase and resell securities to the public either on a firm commitment or best-efforts basis.

underwriting agreement A binding contract between the underwriter and the company that is signed on the day before the stock is sold (also see *letter of intent*).

warrant The right to purchase a security at a specified price, usually within a stipulated time period.

Index